YOUR IDENTITY UPGRADES

YOUR IDENTITY UPGRADES

DISCOVER THE FAST TRACK TO LIVING THE BLESSED LIFE

Tim Concannon

ISBN: 0692588043
ISBN 13: 9780692588048
Library of Congress Control Number: 2015959054
Fresh Fire Publishers, Magnolia, NJ

"Who is it that can tell me who I am?"
—William Shakespeare, *King Lear*, act 1, scene 4

Acknowledgments

I once heard Bill Johnson, the pastor of Bethel Church in Redding, California, say, "If you want to kill giants, then hang out with giant killers." He went on to say that all the giants related to Goliath were killed by people connected to David. My life and my ministry have been shaped by many giants of the faith. I want to thank Pat Robertson, whose ministry led me to the Lord. I would also like to thank Ed Vetkoskey, who faithfully nurtured my faith and confirmed my calling into the ministry; Dan DelVecchio, the great missionary apostle to Spain, who discipled me and trained me to walk in the Spirit; Bill Johnson and Randy Clark, whose writings, impartations, and conferences have radically shaped my life; Dan Mohler, who modeled what kingdom power and love look like on the street; Rob Stoppard, who helped me overcome the wounds of my past and to chart a new course for kingdom living; and Georgian Banov, a true friend and a constant source of inspiration. Each in his own way showed me a better way to live and minister. I can now see the kingdom of God more clearly by standing on the shoulders of these giants.

To my wife, Beth. What can I say but thank you for standing by me while I chased the promise that was put in my heart so long ago. You were willing to take risks and follow me as I pursued the dream of building His kingdom. You have grown into an amazing woman of God with insight, anointing, and discernment. You are my friend, lover, and emotional anchor, who took being a home-maker to new levels. You are the most amazing mother, homeschool teacher, and nurturer that any child could wish for. We all rise and call you blessed.

Endorsements

WHAT A GREAT JOY IT has been to read through each chapter of this truth-revealing book that was compiled from Tim's own journey with God. This revelatory reading experience is one that will change your life as you are called into your true identity. This is not another how to manual, but rather an invitation to seeing your life and your potential in the upgrades that Tim masterfully outlined. You will walk away from each chapter with a heartfelt sense that the promises of God are actually true for your life. We look forward to adding this life empowering study in our Life Legacy Institute!
ROB STOPPARD, Destiny Unlimited International, Mount Joy, PA

Your Identity Upgrades is a book that is desperately needed today. Pastor Tim Concannon, by taking us to the heart of God, takes us to the heart of what it means to be a Christian – a place that we often missed. Using the Bible, great teachers of the past and personal insight and experience, Pastor Tim sounds the trumpet for a fresh understanding of the riches that are ours in Christ. Filled with sound teaching and practical application and served out of his warm loving heart this book will lift your soul and deepen your faith. As a pastor serving Christ and His people for over fifty years I commend this book to you.
PASTOR BOB SANTILLI, American Baptist Churches

I am so thankful for my friend Tim Cocannon's new book. *Your Identity Upgrades.* The truths found in this book are timeless but also straight from the heart of God for this season in Church history. As you read you will be challenged, equipped, and most definitely receive an impartation of God's kindness towards you. For nearly twenty years I have desired to walk in deep fellowship and fruitfulness with God. I have found the truths contained in this book to be foundational but also subjects that one must consistently revisit in our journey here on earth. So my encouragement to you is not only read but be sure to consistently revisit the truths' found in this book.

ABNER SUAREZ, For Such A Time As This, Inc. Dunn, NC
Author, *Creation Reborn*

I have just finished reading *Your Identity Upgrades.* It is fantastic! The content is on target, timely and fascinating. I am excited about recommending this book to many people.

DR. JOHN GROVE, Senior Pastor, Columbus Baptist Church,
Columbus, NJ

More than 40 years ago the Lord called of us to join Him on an incredible journey of discovering who He is and who we are in Him. Pastor Tim Concannon has been and continues to be a very special guide on the journey. His ability to share deep and profound truths in a simple, straight- forward way through personal experience and practical examples has brought us to deeper levels of understanding God, His promises and His love for us. Through this book and teachings we no longer labor under an orphan spirit nor a slave mentality. We have taken our place as co-heirs with Jesus and are accomplishing His purpose for us operating from God's approval.

PASTORS JIM AND PATTI MOFFETT, Co-creators and
Coordinators of the Life Application Bible Seminar and
missionaries, Palmyra, NJ

Your Identity Upgrades is inspiring, uplifting, truthful and visionary. With his clever use of turn of the phrase he makes this book one you will want to reference and reread. May it bring the church into all the fullness God intended.

BOB MCARTHUR, Senior Pastor, Little Flock Church,
Mount Holly, NJ
Author, *Did You Receive The Holy Spirit When You Believed?*

Pastor Tim Concannon has written a much needed book. For too long the human race has struggled to find its true identity. This book will help you know God in a deeper way and through that knowledge will discover your true identity.

JEFF WHISTON, Senior Pastor, Centro de Amistad, Austin, TX

CONTENTS

PROLOGUE

D. L. MOODY, THE GREAT nineteenth-century evangelist and founder of the Moody Bible Institute, used to say that there were two ways to get to heaven: coach and first class. People traveling by coach live by Psalm 56:3: "What time I am afraid, I will trust in Thee." People traveling first class live by Isaiah 12:2: "Behold, God is my salvation, I will trust and be not be afraid." Both seats will get you to heaven, but traveling first class is far superior to coach. Moody had discovered a truth that set him free from a fear-based life. He described this fear-based lifestyle as traveling by coach. His trust in God and faith in His word propelled him to a first-class lifestyle. Each generation of Christians must discover the truths that will set them free from a limited Christian life (coach) and advance them to a first-class lifestyle.

My journey from coach to first class began more than six years ago. For me the issue was my identity in Christ. Looking back, I can see that I was the victim of identity theft by Satan, but God was about to restore my identity in a powerful new way.

I was invited to a pastors' conference in New Orleans in 2008 hosted by Jesse Duplantis. At the end of the conference, the host pastor said he wanted to pray for us as a group of pastors to whom God would impart a spirit of increase to accelerate our walk with

God. He said that many of God's people are stuck and cannot move forward because a host of issues have crippled their walk with God. He said what each one of us needed was a fresh wind of the Holy Spirit to get us unstuck and launch us forward. I came up for prayer, and as soon as the pastor prayed for me, I fell down under the power of the Holy Spirit. While I was down, he kept declaring the word *increase* over me. Every time he said the word, it was as if an electric shock went through me. After spending some quality "carpet time" on the floor, I picked myself up and headed to the airport for my return flight.

When I arrived at the airport, I realized I had forgotten to pre-book my seat assignment. I went to the ticket counter, and I was informed that the only seat available was a middle seat near the back of the plane. Because I am tall, this would not have been my first or second choice. Boarding the plane, I made my way to the back of the plane and was putting my bag in the overhead compartment when the flight attendant tapped me on the shoulder.

"Mr. Concannon, we need your seat; please follow me."

I thought to myself, "Great, now I'm being bumped from this flight, and I'll probably arrive home in the middle of the night."

As we were heading through the first-class section of the plane, she stopped and pointed to a seat. "Today, you will be traveling first class on us. Please be seated." I have no idea why she did that for me, but somehow I sensed the Lord had arranged this. Tears of gratitude came to my eyes for the amazing goodness of my heavenly Father. In my spirit I sensed the Lord saying, "From now on I am going to teach you how to fly first class in my kingdom."

Over these last few years, since that flight home, God has indeed taught me so many truths about flying first class instead of coach in His kingdom. I've experienced that fresh wind of the Holy Spirit, a spirit of increase accelerating my walk with God. In these pages I share my journey of discovery. May these truths accelerate your walk with God to heights you never dreamed of reaching. I believe that by gaining a deeper understanding of your true identity in Christ, you will walk in victories and experience breakthroughs that have long escaped you. May the Spirit of truth enlighten you and empower you to tear down strongholds and traditions that have held you back. So, say good-bye to coach and get ready to be upgraded to first class.

CHAPTER 1

THE FAVORABLE YEAR
OF THE LORD

TRY TO IMAGINE THE SCENE: Jesus had just entered the synagogue of his hometown in Nazareth. News about His amazing ministry had spread far and wide. The miracles He had performed in Capernaum were the talk of everyone in Galilee. There was excitement in the air, and everyone's eyes were fixed on Him as He got up to read. He was handed the scroll of Isaiah, the prophet, and He opened it and began to read: "The Spirit of the Lord is upon Me, because He anointed Me to preach the gospel to the poor. He sent Me to proclaim release to the captives, And recovery of sight to the blind, to set free those who are oppressed, to proclaim the favorable year of the Lord" (Luke 4:18–19). And He closed the scroll, gave it back to the attendant, and sat down; and the eyes of all in the synagogue were fixed on Him. And He began to say to them, "Today this scripture has been fulfilled in your hearing" (Luke 4:20–21). For a brief moment, everyone was amazed at the gracious words He had spoken. But that amazement soon turned to unbelief, as the people could not get past the fact that he was "Joseph's son." How could the carpenter's son claim this messianic mission for Himself? It was one thing to perform miracles in Capernaum but quite another to imply that He was God's anointed one.

Jesus sensed their unbelief and implied that they were too familiar with Him to enter into the blessings that happened in Capernaum. He was a prophet without honor in His own town. He also angered them when He stated that God often had to go outside the nation of Israel to reveal His miraculous power. He used the examples of Naaman the leper and the widow from Zarephath, both Gentiles who had received God's miraculous blessing (Luke 4:24–27). The synagogue members were so incensed by Jesus's statements they drove Him out of the synagogue and tried to throw Him over a cliff. Jesus then had to make a supernatural exit and returned to Capernaum. His great homecoming ended with a great escape.

It saddens me to think about how the people of Nazareth missed the wonderful truths that Jesus was sharing. But we are no different. How often do we step over great riches of revelation in favor of religion or tradition? But looking again at the mission statement that Jesus shared in Nazareth, I have found treasures that have inflamed my heart and staggered my mind.

Let's take a look at how Jesus summarized His mission to mankind. He came to bring good news to the afflicted, to set the captives free, to heal the brokenhearted, and finally to proclaim the favorable year of the Lord. Each one of these statements would require a book to plumb the depth of the revelations that they contain. But I want to draw your attention to the phrase "to proclaim the favorable year of the Lord." For years I always thought it meant that it was simply a good year because Jesus finally came to earth. The fullness of time had come. Soon mankind's sins could be forgiven, and we could receive eternal life. I now know that this one phrase contains one of the greatest revelations of God's redemptive purpose. This revelation provided me with an identity upgrade that changed my life and my ministry.

When Jesus spoke of proclaiming the favorable year of the Lord, He was referring to the "Year of Jubilee." Let's take a look at this Old Testament celebration in Leviticus 25:1–11 and see how it applies to our lives:

> The Lord then spoke to Moses at Mount Sinai, saying, "Speak to the sons of Israel and say to them, 'When you come into the land which I shall give you, then the land shall have a sabbath to the Lord. Six years you shall sow your field, and six years you shall prune your vineyard and gather in its crop, but during the seventh year the land shall have a Sabbath to the Lord; you shall not sow your field or prune your vineyard. 'Your harvest's aftergrowth you shall not reap, and your grapes of the untrimmed vine you shall not gather; the land shall have a sabbatical year. All of you shall have the Sabbath products of the land for food; yourself, and your male and female slaves, and your hired men and your foreign resident, those who live as aliens with you. Even your cattle and the animals that are in the land shall have all its crop to eat. 'You are to count off seven Sabbaths of the years for yourself, seven times seven years, so that you may have a time of seven Sabbaths of years, namely, forty-nine years. You shall then sound a ram's horn abroad on the tenth day of the seventh month; on the day of atonement you shall sound a horn all through the land. You shall thus consecrate the fiftieth year and proclaim a release through the land to all of its inhabitants. It shall be jubilee for you, and each of you shall return to his own property, and each of you shall return to his family."

God provided an economic system by which every seven years the land would have a Sabbath. There would be no farming during that seventh year. God had promised that there would be an abundant harvest during the sixth year to carry His people through the seventh year. After a series of seven of these Sabbaths, namely forty-nine years, a year of Jubilee was proclaimed. The Jubilee was important for two reasons. During that forty-nine-year period, if an Israelite experienced financial hardship, he could sell his land or himself as a hired worker to another landowner to cover his debts. Once Jubilee was declared, all his debts were canceled. He now could get all his land back, and he was restored to his family. Thus, his identity and his land were restored.

Similarly, Jesus came to restore mankind to their true identity as sons and daughters of God and to their abundant inheritance in Him. Jesus is our Jubilee. Our sin debt has been canceled. You are no longer a slave to sin but are set free to live as His child. All the resources of heaven are now at your disposal, and you can rule and reign with Him. It is interesting to note that the Liberty Bell in Philadelphia has Leviticus 25:10 inscribed on the top rim of the bell, and it reads, "Proclaim liberty throughout all the land unto all the inhabitants thereof." This symbol of our nation's freedom carries this wonderful biblical reference. Just as our nation found its new identity and its vast resources, we too can celebrate our newfound identity and resources. To extend the analogy, I should point out that the Liberty Bell rang until it developed a substantial crack in the bell, and then it ceased ringing. In the same way, I feel the church has forgotten to "proclaim liberty" or Jubilee to the saints of God. We have settled for a diminished identity with meager resources.

The story of the prodigal son found in Luke 15:11–32 provides an accurate portrayal of how many Christians live their lives. When the prodigal son returned home after squandering his father's wealth, he freely repented but insisted on living life as one of his father's hired men. The first thing the father did was to restore his son to his true identity. The father gave him a robe, a ring, and new sandals, thus reestablishing his identity as a son. The next thing the father did was prepare a lavish feast for his son. Only the best would do, and the fatted calf was prepared. Paradise lost had now been found. Let the party begin!

Like the prodigal son, we too want to earn our forgiveness and settle for a diminished identity. It seems like the humble thing to do, but it is an insult to grace. Grace is the removal of sin and the restoration of our lost estate. Consider Paul's letter to the Ephesians, in which he describes this same promise:

> He predestined us to adoption as sons through Jesus Christ to Himself, according to the kind intention of His will, to the praise of the glory of His grace, which He freely bestowed on us in the Beloved. In Him we have redemption through His blood, the forgiveness of our trespasses, according to the riches of His grace which He lavished upon us. (Eph. 1:7–8)

True humility is learning how to freely receive what the Father has provided. This restoration, this Jubilee, exalts Him, not us. The expression "to the praise of the glory of His grace" conveys the idea that this grace in which we now stand is a fountain of never-ending praise to the one who offers such grace.

Rejecting our true identity as sons and daughters will always reduce us to the status of hired servants. The older brother in this story never left home but lived his life as a hired servant. He never neglected a command from his father, and he believed that his performance would lead to his identity. The father came out to rescue him from this lie and said, "Son, you have always been with me and all that I have is yours." (Luke 15:31) Notice the father called him "son," not servant, and reminded him that as a son, all of the father's wealth belonged to him. True identity will always release heaven's resources.

A number of years ago, I was preaching on the story of the prodigal son, and when I came to the father's declaration, "Son, you have always been with me, and all that I have is yours," I started weeping in the pulpit, and I could barely stop. It was as if I were hearing those words for the first time. After serving the Lord for many years, my relationship with God was more like an employer-employee relationship. One day when I was praying—or maybe begging God—about some pressing needs in the church, He spoke to me and said, "Tim, why don't you talk to me as a son?" The sad truth was that I didn't know how to talk to Him as a son. I was coming to God as if He were the shop steward and I were simply presenting Him with a requisition slip for more souls, more money, and more energy. That one question—"Why don't you talk to me as a son?"—haunted me. It was not the first time the Lord wanted me to embrace this idea that I was His son, not just His servant.

While working as a missionary in Spain early in my ministry, I was reading the story of Jesus's baptism. I came to the part where the heavens opened and the Father declared, "This is my beloved Son in whom I am well pleased." I sensed the Lord saying to me, "Tim, claim this for yourself." I instantly rejected that thought as blasphemy. I could never compare myself to Jesus. I could readily understand the Father's validation of Jesus, but my sins and failures instantly disqualified me from such an honor. Like the older brother, I went back to the harvest fields trying to obey His commands and maybe one day earn His validation. How many years I wasted trying to earn what was already mine!

Many of us have lived our lives as second-class citizens of the kingdom of God. It sounds so spiritual and humble to declare, "I'm just a poor lowly sinner." Nothing could be further from the truth. The good news of the kingdom is that you are now a son or a daughter, and all that the Father has is yours! To minimize our true identity in Christ is an insult to the enormous price He paid for our redemption. The Father's mission was to send His Son, who proclaimed liberty, to those who had lost their identity and their inheritance: "The Son of Man has come to seek and to save *that* which was lost" (Luke 19:10, emphasis added). The word "redeem" means to buy back. That is what Jesus did when He shed His blood for us. He redeemed us and bought back our lost estate. What mankind had in the garden, unbroken fellowship with God and dominion in the natural, is now ours again.

When the year of Jubilee finally arrived, it commenced with great fanfare: "You shall then sound the ram's horn abroad on the tenth of the seventh month; on the Day of Atonement you shall sound the ram's horn all through your land" (Lev. 25:9). Imagine yourself in Israel at that time. Thousands of people had gone into debt and had lost their property and their identities. They were working as servants for other landowners. Suddenly they heard the sound of the ram's horn. Jubilee had arrived. A day of atonement was declared. All debts were paid. Their property and identities were now restored. They could all go back home. What had been lost would now be recovered. Thousands of people traveled to their ancestral homes rejoicing. The sounds of laughter, music, and celebration resounded throughout the land.

For the Christian, Jesus's atonement has accomplished the same thing. His sacrifice has paid our debts, and we can rejoice in our new standing as sons and daughters of the living God. All the resources of heaven are now ours. Peter describes these resources as having "everything pertaining to life and godliness" (2 Pet. 1:3). The challenge for the church is to "sound the ram's horn" and to boldly proclaim to the church and to a lost world the favorable year of the Lord.

So often the church has simply presented the gospel as a vehicle to get out of hell and to secure your place in heaven. There is nothing wrong with this; eternal life is the ultimate prize. However, Jesus also came to restore and redeem all things. Mankind can once again taste the life that God originally planned from the beginning. The church should be a visual aid to show the world what restored humanity should look like. Once we embrace our true identities as sons and daughters of the living God and learn how to access all His resources, we can bring heaven to earth. This was the life that Jesus lived, and He invites all of us to follow Him.

SIN CONSCIOUSNESS VERSUS SON CONSCIOUSNESS

ARE YOU A SINNER OR a saint? Often when I speak at churches, I ask this question. More often than not, most people identify themselves as sinners. How we see ourselves directly affects the way we live our life. That is why we must settle once and for all our true spiritual identity. If the Bible declares us saints, why do we persist in identifying ourselves as sinners? Why is it so hard to come into agreement with what the word of God says about our true identity as saints? I think the reason is that we were so used to sinning before our conversion that when we fall into sin as Christians we unconsciously assume that our sin nature is still intact. It also doesn't help that our churches still reaffirm the label of sinner to all the saints of God. I believe we are on the verge of a major theological shift in which the people of God can finally live in agreement with the Bible's declaration of their true spiritual identity. Let the eyes of your understanding be enlightened as we examine the following scriptures.

2 CORINTHIANS 5:17

"If any man is in Christ he is a new creation, the old has passed away and all things are becoming new." With these words, the apostle Paul proclaims that something radical happened to you when you were born again. When Christ died, you died with Him. When Christ was buried, you were buried with Him, and when Christ arose, you rose with Him. Your sin nature was put to death on the cross with Him. You are now seated with Him in heavenly places. You have the righteousness of Christ as your own. You are now a saint and a son. If you sin, it is not out of your sin nature because that nature was put to death. The power of sin has been broken, but the habit of sin remains. You may yield to your flesh, but sin is no longer master over you. The problem lies in the fact that our unrenewed minds keep us trapped with the false identity of sinners. To fully appreciate this radical transformation from sinner to saint, it is imperative that we look at the many verses that confirm this truth.

ROMANS 6:3–11

Or do you not know that all of us who have been baptized into Christ Jesus have been baptized into His death? Therefore we have been buried with Him through baptism into death, so that as Christ was raised from the dead through the glory of the Father, so we too might walk in newness of life. For if we become united with Him in the likeness of His death, certainly we shall also be in the likeness of His resurrection, knowing this, that our old self was crucified with Him, in order that our body of sin might be done away with, so that we would no longer be slaves to sin; for he who has died is freed from sin. Now if we have died with Christ, we believe that we shall also live with Him. Knowing that Christ, having been raised from the dead, is never to die again; death no longer is master over Him. For the death that He died, He died to sin once for all; but the life that He lives, He lives to God. Even so consider yourselves dead to sin, but alive to God in Christ Jesus.

This is how the passage is presented in the Message translation:

Could it be any clearer? Our old way of life nailed to the cross with Christ; a decisive end to that sin-miserable life— no longer at sin's every beck and call! What we believe is this: if we get included in Christ's sin-conquering death, we also get included in his life-saving resurrection. We know that when Jesus was raised from the dead it was a signal of the end of death-as-the-end. Never again will death have the last word. When Jesus died He took sin down with him, but alive he brings God down to us. From now on think of it this way: Sin speaks a dead language that means nothing to you; God speaks your mother tongue, and you hang on to every word. You are dead to sin and alive to God. That's what Jesus did.

We can enhance our understanding of this remarkable truth by focusing on two words found in verses 6 and 11 of this chapter.

Romans 6:6 says, "Knowing this that our old self was crucified with Him." The word "knowing" implies a gradual understanding, or we could say that "we have come to know" that our old self was crucified. This "knowing" is a destination where every Christian should finally arrive. Our freedom from the dominion of sin depends on it. I believe that we have trouble grasping this fact because of the temptations we face and the sins we commit. We conclude that our old sinful nature is alive and kicking. Here we must differentiate between our old sinful nature and the flesh. The desires of the flesh are not the same as having a sin nature. The moment you realize your sin nature is dead, the faster you will overcome sin. Paul verifies this fact when he says, "Sin shall not be master over you" (Rom. 6:14).

Romans 6:11 states, "Even so consider yourselves to be dead to sin, but alive to God in Christ Jesus." The word "consider" implies a solid fact. It is similar to an accounting term. When money is credited to your account, you can be certain that those funds are available. We now take our lives out of the debit column of sin and place ourselves in the credit column of righteousness. Know for certain, for sure, that you are dead to sin and alive to God. This is your true identity.

For most of us, these truths are hard to grasp. I once heard about an illustration used by Watchman Nee to amplify this point. He was a Chinese pastor who had a powerful ministry before the communists took over and imprisoned him. To highlight the truth that when Christ died you also died, Watchman Nee took a Chinese dollar (yaun) and placed it in a book. He then burned the book in front of the congregation and then asked everyone what happened to the dollar (yaun). The obvious answer is that the bill was burned with the book. He went on to explain that this is what happened to us. God put you in Christ on the cross. When He died, you died. Your sin nature was put to death.

LET US LOOK AT COLOSSIANS 3:1–5

Therefore if you have been raised up with Christ, keep seeking the things above, where Christ is, seated at the right hand of God. Set your minds on things above, not on the things of the earth. For you have died and your life is now hidden with Christ in God. When Christ, who is our life, is revealed, then you also will be revealed with Him in glory. Therefore consider the members of your earthly body as dead to immorality, impurity, passion, evil desire, and greed which amounts to idolatry.

Paul again emphasizes that we are dead to sin. Stop calling yourself a sinner. That is not your identity. You may struggle with sin and the flesh, but that is not who you are. The fact that you have remorse or regret for your actions tells you that sin is not your true identity.

Every week I minister at a faith-based drug rehabilitation program in Philadelphia. It breaks my heart to see the ravages of alcoholism and drug addiction. Many of these men have been through other programs based on the twelve-step program used by Alcoholics Anonymous. In this program, you begin by identifying yourself as an alcoholic. That is step one. Nothing is wrong with coming into agreement with your real problem. To confess means to come into agreement. The underlying problem is trying to overcome addiction by identifying yourself as an addict. I tell these men that they are saints fighting addiction. We see more breakthroughs when these individuals finally believe who they really are.

ONE FINAL CONSIDERATION IS HEBREWS 12:1–2

Therefore, since we have so great a cloud of witnesses surrounding us, let us also lay aside every encumbrance and the sin which easily entangles us, and let us run with endurance the race that is set before us. Fixing our eyes on Jesus the author and perfecter of faith, who for the joy set before Him endured the cross, despising the shame, and has sat down at the right hand of the throne of God.

The writer of Hebrews provides a road map to follow in embracing our true identity. He tells us to fix our eyes on Jesus. The principle is clear. What you focus on is what you become. The more you focus on your new nature, the more you empower that reality. The opposite is also true. The more you focus on your sins, the more you will empower the flesh. You will have an unconscious expectation to sin because you believe that is who you really are. Jesus is the author of our faith. As you focus on Him, He creates greater faith in your new identity. His death on the cross was a victory over sin for you. Focus on that victory. Don't focus on the sin you committed or on the lie that you have a sin nature. That perspective will rob you of the faith you need to overcome sin and the flesh.

The church's preoccupation with sin consciousness is directly connected with our focus on leading someone to Christ. Sin is the problem that separates people from God, and we must challenge all who come to Christ to repent of their sins and be baptized. Evangelical churches have been extremely effective in leading people to a saving knowledge of Jesus Christ. Many church services end with an altar call inviting unbelievers to come forward to deal with their sins. This practice began in earnest during the revivals in the eighteenth and nineteenth centuries. People were challenged to come forward to the "mourners' bench" to examine their spiritual condition. This was especially true in the meetings of the great nineteenth-century revivalist Charles Finney. From the mourners' bench, sinners were led to making a commitment of their life to Christ. Out of that model evolved the altar call. You may have seen this in a Billy Graham crusade or some other type of large evangelistic meeting.

Today most evangelical churches include an altar call at the end of the service. In some circles, there is an altar call every week. Our church culture has put the focus on sin and the need to get right with God. Unfortunately, we tend to group the lost and the saved together in the same invitation. The original mourners' bench was designed just for those who were unsure of their standing with God and was a challenge to repent. For the unsaved, sin is the issue, and repentance is a requirement for salvation. Getting right with God is the language of sin consciousness. If we are addressing the lost, this is fine, but we tend to gather sinners and saints in the same basket. If the altar call is the final destination for every service, then we invariably design each sermon to focus on sinful behavior and thus invite everyone to come forward. Nothing is wrong with repentance. We all need to respond to the convicting ministry of the Holy Spirit in this regard. My point is that we do not spend the necessary time instructing church members of their true standing before God. Outside of Christ, we are sinners. Once inside of Christ, we are saints. We are the sons and daughters of the living God who are now washed, justified, and glorified.

To see ourselves clearly as sons and daughters of God, all we have to do is look at how the apostle Paul begins each of his letters to the various churches. He usually starts by saying, "To the saints," not "to the sinners." Let us look at his various salutations (the emphasis in these quotations is mine):

- **Romans 1:6–7**: "Among whom you also are *the called* of Jesus Christ; to all who are *beloved* of God in Rome, *called as saints*"
- **1 Corinthians 1:2**: "*To the church* of God which is in Corinth, to those *who have been sanctified* in Christ Jesus, *saints by calling...*"
- **2 Corinthians 1:1**: "*To the church* of God which is at Corinth with *all the saints* who are throughout Achaia..."
- **Philippians 1:1**: "To *all the saints* in Christ Jesus who are Philippi..."

* **Colossians 1:2:** "To *the saints* and faithful brethren in Christ who are at Colossae..."

We all need to embrace what our true identity is before God. The more comfortable we are as saints, the easier it will be for us to reject sin.

Bold Declarations

Historically the church has had multiple creeds or confessions that have anchored our theology. Two of the most popular are the Nicene Creed and the Apostles' Creed. Both creeds highlight the divinity of Christ and His mission on earth. I think the church today needs some kind of creed to cement in our hearts and minds our true standing before God. We must elevate son consciousness over sin consciousness. Over the last few years, I have tried sum up my identity and standing with God in this way:

My Declaration of Sonship

Father, because of the sacrifice of your Son for me, I am now the righteousness of Christ. I am holy and blameless and without reproach. I have been made perfect by the blood shed for me. You have purified my heart by faith, and I am now a new creation. I am now dead to sin and alive to You. I am now washed, sanctified, and justified by your Spirit. I am seated with you in heavenly places, and I have confident access to the throne of grace for all my needs. You have called me your son, and I can walk in newness of life through your Son, Jesus Christ (2 Cor. 5:21; Col. 1:22; Heb. 10:14; Acts 15:9; 2 Cor. 5:17; Rom. 6:11; 1 Cor. 6:11; Eph. 2:6; Eph. 3:12; Gal. 4:6; Rom. 6:4).

You and I must renew our minds in these truths to walk in our redeemed nature. Once we are born again, our spirits are new, but our minds have to be renewed. We must take the time to immerse ourselves in these truths that transform. If we keep reminding saints that they are sinners, then they will live like sinners. If the messages from our pulpits are veiled in condemnation, guilt, and shame, they reinforce a warped identity and give us no platform to have victory over sin. Son consciousness will give us that platform to live victoriously.

What about sin? Satan uses our failures to rob us of our true identity. He wants to reinforce who we are not. "You can't be a son if you did *that*," he yells in our ears. He wants you to come into agreement with him to live a life of defeat. It seems as though we can never win. We have both the church and Satan reminding us that we are sinners. We must fight for our true identity as sons and daughters. Anytime we sin, we have an advocate with the Father, Jesus Christ the righteous, who has promised to cleanse us from *all* unrighteousness when we confess our sins. If all unrighteousness is gone, what is left? Only righteousness! Our true standing before God! Hallelujah!

So if you sin, quickly confess your sin and continue to walk in your true identity as a son or daughter of the living God who is pursuing holiness in the fear of God.

God and Satan See You the Same

One of the most remarkable truths of our new standing with God is that both Satan and God see us the same. God sees us as His sons and daughters who are designed to live in fellowship with Him and live victoriously while here on earth. Our Father in heaven desperately wants us to know these truths. Satan also sees us this way and fights just as hard so that we never know these truths. If Satan can bury us in sin consciousness, we will never embrace our full potential. He is the "accuser of the brethren" and works overtime to take from us our true, confident standing before our heavenly Father. Satan fears an enlightened saint who knows his or her true position before God and his or her authority over the enemy.

What about My Sin Nature?

This may seem radical to some, but you no longer have a sin nature. The results of His suffering and death are astounding. Jesus conquered sin and death, and His victory is now our victory. Because of this victory, He put our sin nature to death and made us alive together with Him. Listen to the New Testament description of our present standing before God: "We are the righteousness of Christ" (2 Cor. 5:17). "We are now holy, blameless and beyond reproach" (Col. 1:22).

The writer of Hebrews paints one of the most glowing portraits of our new identity. Take a look at the following three verses that clearly show the end of your sin nature and your true standing before God:

- "He has been manifested to put away sin by the sacrifice of Himself" (Heb. 9:26).
- "We have been made holy through the sacrifice of the body of Jesus Christ once for all" (Heb. 10:10).
- "For by one sacrifice he has made perfect forever those who are being made holy" (Heb. 10:14).

Have you ever considered yourself as holy and perfect? Remember God's words to Peter in Acts 10:15: "Do not call anything impure that God has made clean." Why keep calling yourself a sinner when God made you a saint?

Trying to resist sin when you believe you are a sinner is practically impossible. On the other hand, when you know you are righteous, you can wage war against the flesh and be confident in your victory. The apostle Peter says, "The Lord knows how to rescue the godly from temptation" (2 Pet. 2:9). Are you godly or ungodly? The real key to victory is knowing that sin is not the problem; rather, it is our lack of understanding of our true identity as righteous sons and daughters. It is so much easier to go to the throne of grace when we are confident in our righteous standing before God. Then we can apprehend all the grace and mercy we need to continue to live a victorious life. Then we have free, unhindered access to God. In fact, we have the same access to the Father that Jesus had when He walked the earth.

CHAPTER 3

GRATEFULLY DEAD

IT IS IMPORTANT TO LOOK at further revelations that confirm the reality of our being alive to God and dead to sin. Paul touches on these points in almost every letter he wrote to the early churches. It may seem repetitious, but because Paul amplified these truths, we need to keep looking until we finally see. Here are a few well-known verses that need to be clearly understood: "For you have died and your life is hidden with Christ in God" (Col. 3:3). "I have been crucified with Christ and it is no longer I who live but Christ lives in me" (Gal. 2:20). Paul is saying that it is finally time to have a funeral for your old sin nature once and for all. Doing this requires faith to believe this is true. Take the time to meditate on these verses until you can see the amazing work that God has done for you with regard to sin. Consider the way many Christians speak today; you would not think that anything has happened to their old nature.

Some call the book of Romans the Grand Canyon of the New Testament. Granted, it is very deep, but it is not unknowable. In chapters 6, 7, and 8, we receive major revelations of our new standing before God and of how to overcome the flesh. The problem for many believers is chapter 7. Many people believe Paul is talking about his current redeemed state. However, the struggle Paul is referring to occurred when he was still under the law as a Pharisee, not after he assumed his new standing with Christ. You often hear believers quote Romans 7:19: "For the good that I want, I do not do, but I practice the very evil that I do not want." They believe their struggle is clear evidence that they have two competing natures. It is easy to understand their conclusion. Because we struggle with sin, we think the sin nature was never dealt a deathblow at Calvary. However, in Romans 6, 7, and 8, the words "dead," "death," "die," or "died" appear more than thirty times. You would think we would finally wrap our minds around the fact that we are really, truly, and permanently dead.

Paul makes this very useful analogy found in Romans 7:1–3:

> Or do you not know, brethren (for I am speaking to those who know the law), that the law has jurisdiction over a person as long as he lives? For the married woman is bound by law to her husband while he is living; but if her husband dies she is released from the law concerning her husband. So then, if while her husband is living she is joined to another man, she shall be called an adulteress; but if her husband dies, she is free from the law, so that she is not an adulteress though she is joined to another man.

He compares our old sin nature as being married to the law. Whenever a spouse died, you were free to marry another. The law was like an abusive spouse that ruthlessly controlled us; "the power of sin is in the law" (1 Cor. 15:56). However, we died to the law when Christ died. Therefore, the power of sin is dead. We are now married to Christ because we are His bride, and we are free to live through Him.

Let's revisit Romans 6:5–7: "For if we have become united with Him in the likeness of His death, certainly we shall also be in the likeness of His resurrection, knowing this, that our old self was cru-cified with Him, in order that our body of sin might be done away with, so that we would no longer be slaves to sin. For he who has died is free from sin."

Many saints are in the grave-robbing business. We are always digging up and trying to resuscitate the old nature. Listen to how you verbalize your struggle with the flesh. Ask yourself how many times you refer to the flesh as the old nature. Our own words betray us because the church is still teaching that we have two natures. It is a form of Christian schizophrenia.

Consider Paul's celebration of our new nature and our new free-dom over sin: "For if while we were enemies we were reconciled to God through the death of His Son, it is much more (certain), now that we are reconciled, that we should be saved (daily delivered from sin's dominion) through His (resurrection) life" (Rom. 5:10, AMP). To paraphrase this thought, if God died for you while you were His enemy, how much more will He do for you now that you and He are friends, even family? Grace now reigns through righ-teousness. His death created a permanent barrier between your old sin nature and the life you now have in the spirit.

If Romans 7 describes our true condition, if I can't do the good I want to, then I am saying that sin is greater than the spirit and that I am incapable of living a victorious Christian life. The point of Romans 6 and 8 is that we have the victory over sin because God put us on the cross with Christ. We have become disconnected from the power source of sin forever.

In Romans 8:2, Paul states that "the law of the spirit of life in Christ Jesus has set us free from the law of sin and death." We all understand natural laws. If you want to overcome the law of gravity, you need a greater law to accomplish this feat. The laws of lift and thrust will overcome gravity. These laws give us the ability to fly in airplanes. The same is true in the spirit realm. A greater law is now at work in your life. Stop believing in the lesser law of sin and celebrate the greater law of the spirit of life in Christ Jesus. The more you know you are dead, the more you will live in the spirit.

Try wrapping your faith around these two pillars of freedom: when Christ died, you died, and an actual, literal law has set you free from the law of sin and death.

CHAPTER 4

IDENTITY FIRST, BEHAVIOR SECOND

"PUT ON THE LORD JESUS Christ and make no provision for the flesh in regards to its lust" (Rom. 13:14). In this one small verse, the apostle Paul gives us a road map to a truly empowered life. Notice the order in which he challenges us to walk in righteousness. "Put on the Lord Jesus" is first; "making no provision for the flesh" is second. Identity first, behavior second. We must follow this pattern. For most of my Christian life, I had these concepts reversed. I was always trying to deny the flesh to establish my identity. In every church culture, the pressure to conform to accepted Christian behavior is enormous. Embracing behavior at the expense of our identity is very easy. No one will question your identity as long as you live by the accepted behavioral code. This is just another trap of the enemy to make us live under the law rather than grace.

One day when Jesus was walking through Jericho, he saw Zaccheus sitting up in a tree (Luke 19:1–10). He called for him, "Zaccheus, hurry and come down, for today I must stay at your house." Zaccheus hurried and came down and gladly welcomed Him. The crowd was horrified. "Doesn't He know that this man is a sinner?" they reasoned. Jesus knew exactly who Zaccheus was and knew that his greatest need was to be adopted as a son. He needed an identity fix, not a behavioral fix.

What changed Zaccheus's behavior? Was it a lecture on the law or an outpouring of grace and acceptance? Was it a celebration as a son or a condemnation as a sinner? Look at the result of Jesus approaching this man as a son. Zaccheus gave half of what he had to the poor, and if he had defrauded anyone, he repaid four times as much. Generosity replaced greed because identity replaced behavior.

Jesus knew that the key to unlocking our potential for righteousness was adoption. He came to seek and to save that which was lost. What man lost in the garden was his true identity. Sin had broken that link, and we had all become sinners; but now that Jesus has come, He has restored us once again as His sons and daughters. Listen to Jesus at the end of this story: "Today salvation has come to this house, because he, too, is a son of Abraham." Salvation through adoption is the hope of mankind.

HOW THE BIBLE DESCRIBES OUR IDENTITY

For us to appreciate the centrality of establishing our identity before we tackle our behavior, reflect on the following passages of scripture.

EPHESIANS 5:1–3

"Therefore be imitators of God, as beloved children; and walk in love, just as Christ also loved you and gave Himself up for us, an offering and a sacrifice to God as a fragrant aroma. But immorality or any impurity or greed must not even be named among you, as is proper among saints."

EPHESIANS 5:8–11

"For you were formerly darkness, but now you are Light in the Lord; walk as children of Light (for the fruit of Light consists in all goodness and righteousness and truth), trying to learn what is pleasing to the Lord. Do not participate in the unfruitful deeds of darkness but instead even expose them."

GALATIANS 4:6–11

"Because you are sons, God has sent forth the Spirit of His Son into our hearts, crying, "Abba! Father!" Therefore you are no longer a slave, but a son, and if a son, then an heir through God. However at that time, when you did not know God, you were slaves to those which by nature are no gods. But now that you have come to know God, or rather to be known by God, how is it that you turn again to the weak and worthless elemental things, to which you desire to be enslaved all over again?"

COLOSSIANS 3:1–5

"Therefore if you have been raised up with Christ, keep seeking the things above, where Christ is, seated at the right hand of God. Set your mind on the things above, not on the things that are on the earth. For you have died and your life is hidden with Christ in God. When Christ, who is our life, is revealed, then you also will be revealed with Him in glory. Therefore consider the members of your earthly body as dead to immorality, impurity, passion, evil desire, and greed which amounts to idolatry."

COLOSSIANS 3:9–10

"Do not lie to one another, since you laid aside the old self with its evil practices, and have put on the new self who is being renewed to a true knowledge according to the image of the one who created him."

1 PETER 2:9–11

"But you are A CHOSEN RACE, A royal PRIESTHOOD, A HOLY NATION, A PEOPLE FOR GOD's OWN POSSESSION, so that you may proclaim the excellencies of Him who has called you out of darkness into His marvelous light; for you were once NOT A PEOPLE, but now you are THE PEOPLE OF GOD; you had NOT RECEIVED MERCY, but now you have RECEIVED MERCY. Beloved, I urge you as aliens and strangers to abstain from the fleshly lusts that wage war against the soul."

1 JOHN 3:1–3

"See how great a love the Father has bestowed on us, that we should be called children of God; and such we are. For this reason the world does not know us, because it did not know Him. Beloved, now we are children of God, and it has not appeared as yet what we will be. We know that when He appears, we will be like Him, because we will see Him just as He is. And everyone who has this hope fixed on Him purifies himself, just as He is pure."

YOUR BEHAVIOR DOES NOT DEFINE YOU

Throughout the New Testament, you see the link between identity and behavior. For most Christians, this is a difficult challenge because the tendency is to put behavior ahead of identity. Their redeemed identity seems more elusive in light of their sin. Not only do they struggle with their own sense of sin, but they also have Satan, the accuser of the brethren, amplifying their failures. We must let the word of God speak louder than our own thoughts and the lies of the enemy.

When they sin, most Christians feel a sense of failure and remorse. Why is that? Because they know that the sin is inconsistent with their Christian lives. Actually, feeling remorse is a telltale sign that your sinful behavior is not your real identity. Simply confess your sin and "put on the Lord Jesus Christ." Learn to appropriate Jesus as your ally in your battle against the flesh. We fight from identity, not for identity. All the armor mentioned in Ephesians 6 is nothing more than a picture of putting on Jesus—your new identity.

CHAPTER 5

NEW IDENTITY REQUIRES NEW THINKING

"DO NOT BE CONFORMED TO this world but be transformed by the renewing of the mind" (Rom. 12:2). When you received Jesus Christ into your heart, you were born again, and your spirit came alive. The Holy Spirit bore witness with your spirit that you were now a child of God. The problem is not with our hearts but with our heads. Sometimes I think that the church needs a holy decapitation to help us come into alignment with our true identity. This is why it is so important to have our minds renewed in truth: to set us free from the old way we looked at ourselves and at God.

For many Christians, being born again and going to heaven is enough. They celebrate the gift of eternal life but have little impact on the world around them. Their identity is wrapped up in the fact that they are saved. For many people, the study of the Bible is a pursuit of information, but rarely does that information turn into a revelation of who they really are. They are aware of the stories, the doctrines, and the commands of the word but are deficient in capturing the big picture of Christlikeness. The big picture of the New Testament is that Jesus became you so that you could become Him. You can now relate to the Father as a son, the same way Jesus did. "I go to My Father and your Father" (John 20:17). You can also manifest the same life as Jesus did while He walked the earth. "The works I do, you shall do also" (John 14:12).

The area of mind renewal must first begin with a demolition project. Reflect on Paul's clear instruction in 2 Corinthians 10:5: "We are destroying speculations and every lofty thing raised up against the knowledge of God, and we are taking every thought captive to the obedience of Christ." The antidote for all deception and lies is the truth. Satan is the father of lies. We have to choose which father will shepherd us: the father of lies or our heavenly Father. Jesus said that if we continue in the truth, we will be His disciples and we will know the truth, which will set us free. We must continue in the truth.

We have been adopted into God's family, and yet many of us still struggle to rest in our new adopted home. Many believers live as if God will haul us back to the orphanage any time we fail. Because we are never secure of our true standing in Christ, the enemy will put pressure on us to earn our standing with God. This is the fruit of an orphan spirit married to a spirit of religion. We find ourselves on the treadmill of religious activity trying to prove our value to God. Each time we fail, we try to run harder, but the prize continually eludes us because we are always one sin away from losing our standing in the kingdom. Many churches are nothing more than sanctified orphanages, with orphans singing about an identity that continually eludes them and about a Father they do not really know. Hoping to be truly adopted, each week they promise to try harder for what is already theirs.

We have to marinate our minds in the truths of sonship. We must read the New Testament again and again and confess out loud our true standing before the Father. In church one Sunday, I had the congregation confess together from Colossians 1:22, "I am holy and blameless and without reproach." I then asked everyone if they felt comfortable confessing this truth. To many this was speaking in "strange tongues." The truth is that we are not comfortable walking in grace. The law is always tugging on our sleeve. We usually return to those verses that speak of drifting away or not remaining steadfast so we can put the emphasis on our exclusion and our effort.

I remember a time while I was working in Spain that I was drowning in a sense of self-loathing. I began an unfruitful journey of introspection. All my motives for serving the Lord as a missionary were suspect. I actually began to think that the worse I felt about myself, the more I would please God. Romans 7:18, which begins with "For I know that nothing good dwells in me," became one of the proof texts for my utter unworthiness. I think that the misunderstanding of Romans 7 has tripped up many believers in their secure standing with their heavenly Father, a topic that I will discuss later. There was no obvious sin in my life. I wasn't under conviction for any behavior. It seemed the holy thing to do was to marginalize my standing before God. This is another subtle trap of the enemy because he will convince you that to be humble you must devalue yourself continually. Celebrating your true standing will be perceived as pride. Watch out for that trap.

One day as I was walking through our mission compound, I overheard a brother sharing a verse from Proverbs 8:30: "And I was daily His delight, rejoicing always before Him." It was as if a great shaft of light broke through the darkness surrounding my soul. I didn't remembered reading that verse or hearing it preached. Truth came to my rescue. A moment before, I had been convinced that I was "daily His disappointment," but now the word of God declared that I was "daily His delight." I was overwhelmed by His love and His smile.

Beware of focusing on you and your behavior rather than fixing your eyes on Him.

Turn Your Thinking Around

Here is a short exercise we can all practice.

Begin to confess the truth that you are daily His delight, and let the spirit of adoption once again capture your heart. Renew your mind in this blessed reality. If God needs to speak with you about some issue, He can and will speak to you. Do not go on endless fishing expeditions looking for dirt. This is not the way of the kingdom.

Being rooted and grounded in love is essential for walking in our true identity. Accepted in the beloved is our true address. Many of us play the old game of "He loves me, He loves me not," depending on the circumstances of our day. I got a raise; He loves me. I lost my job; He loves me not. I prayed and studied my Bible today; He loves me. I fell into sin; He loves me not. Round and round we go, never sure of our secure standing. Once again, the focus is directed to our behavior rather than to His covenant love.

David lived his life secure in God's love, and he ended Psalm 23 with these words: "*surely* goodness and lovingkindness will follow me all the days of my life and I will dwell in the house of the Lord forever" (emphasis mine). Your heavenly Father desperately wants you to dwell in His house as a son or a daughter. His perfect love will cast out fear: the fear that you are not good enough and the fear that His grace is not sufficient to overcome any sin in your life. Believe His love. Confess His love. Abide in His love, and joyfully live for Him.

CHAPTER 6

DOMINION THROUGH SACRIFICE

"*YOU ARE A CHOSEN RACE*, a royal priesthood, a holy nation, a people for God's own possession, so that *you may* proclaim the excellencies of Him who has called you out of darkness into His marvelous light" (1 Pet. 2:9, emphasis mine).

This is arguably one of the most amazing descriptions of our status as believers in Jesus Christ. Each phrase is pregnant with manifold revelations. Peter again reinforces the correct pattern of living an effective Christian life: "You are…so that you may." Identity always precedes behavior. But what I want us to focus on is the phrase "a royal priesthood." Here our identity is centered on the fact that we are royalty. To be royal implies that you are connected to a king and a kingdom and to all the resources of that kingdom. This reality should influence how you conduct yourself here on earth. God gave Adam dominion over the earth when He created him. Now that we have come into union with the King of Kings, we are once again called to take dominion and let His kingdom come to earth as it is in heaven.

Many Christians suffer from an inferiority complex. More aware of their sins than their righteousness, they are paralyzed from ruling as kings and priests. They do not believe that they are worthy enough to reign. It also hinders them from believing in the surpassing greatness of His power that is available for them to reign. When we look at the book of Acts, the reputation of the church was that of men "who turned the world upside down." Where are these men today? It often seems that the world has turned the church upside down.

We need to intercede the same way the church did when the Jewish leaders tried intimidation and fear to quiet the church. "Give us more boldness," they cried. The church didn't take note of their threats but told the Lord to take note of them, as if to say, "Check out these guys. Do they have any idea who they are messing with? We have God on our side, so Lord, more boldness, please—and while you're at it, extend your hand to heal and let signs and wonders take place through the name of your holy servant Jesus." Knowing who you are is the most freeing reality on earth. You are royalty, and all that the King of Kings has is yours.

To further amplify our royal standing, Jesus said that the ruler of this age has been cast out. Satan is no longer in control, but we are. I can only imagine the joy that Jesus felt when He was watching Satan fall from heaven like lightning. All authority has been given to us. All means *all*. We are like police officers walking the beat arresting Satan every time we catch him trying to lie, kill, or destroy. Satan is like a bad tenant who needs to be evicted. The tragedy is that the church does not believe it has the power to force his eviction. We do and we must! In Martin Luther's classic hymn "A Mighty Fortress Is Our God," I love the following verse:

And though this world, with devils filled, should threaten to undo us
We will not fear, for God has willed His truth to triumph thro' us

The prince of darkness grim, we tremble not for him, His rage we can endure

For lo his doom is sure: one little word shall fell him.

Look at the confidence of these words. They came from a man confident in his authority, a man confident in his position, a man who shook the known religious world to its foundations. You see the same boldness in Peter and John when they stood before the council after healing the lame beggar. Like Esther, we too have come to royalty for such a time as this. We are God's visual aid to show what mankind was designed to look like.

Not only are we royalty, but we are also priests to our God. The main function of priests in the Old Testament was to offer sacrifices. Under the law there were many prescribed sacrifices or offerings that the nation of Israel was required to offer. The five main offerings or sacrifices that the Lord required were the burnt offering, the grain offering, the peace offering, the sin offering, and the trespass offering. This does not include the daily sacrifices the priest made to the Lord or the special sacrifices that were required on the Day of Atonement. The center of Jewish life was the temple, and it was the center for all these sacrifices. We too are the temple of the Holy Spirit, and He is still looking for the sacrifices that the New Testament priests are required to offer.

THE LIVING SACRIFICE

As royal priests in the New Testament, we offer sacrifices that are the keys to reigning in life. The first sacrifice I want us to look at is the "living sacrifice." Every time we walk in obedience to the word of God and to the leadings of the Holy Spirit, we extend His kingdom. His reign follows our sacrifice. Romans 12:1 highlights this truth: "Therefore I urge you, brethren, by the mercies of God, to present your bodies a living and holy sacrifice, acceptable to God, which is your spiritual service of worship."

The first area of dominion we need to secure is our dominion over sin and the flesh. We have the sure word of God that sin is no longer master over us. When I willingly present my body to God and choose to deny myself, sin no longer has the upper hand in my life. The more we make this choice to present our bodies as a living sacrifice, the easier it is to walk in holiness. There is a multiplier effect in our choices. If I choose unrighteousness, it will result in further unrighteousness, but if I choose the path of righteousness, it will result in freedom from sin and expand holiness in my life.

One of the great by-products of being a living sacrifice is that we disarm Satan and his accusations. He no longer has a foothold to rob us of our confidence before God. He turns every failure into a fiery dart to condemn us. His strategy is to remind us that we are really sinners and not saints and that sin is still a master in our life. We render the accuser of the brethren mute when we choose to walk in holiness and truth. Dominion through sacrifice must be our counterattack against his relentless lies.

Our witness to the world is also rooted in the principle of dominion through sacrifice. If I know that my life is not my own and that I have been bought with a price, I will willingly lay down my life for the cause of Christ. The apostle John further illuminates this truth. Revelation 12:11 says, "And they overcame him by the blood of the Lamb and the word of their testimony and *they did not love their life even when faced with death*" (emphasis mine). When we love the cause of Christ more than ourselves, we can now witness freely. We can approach people who are sick in the streets, pray for them, and not worry about rejection because we are living sacrifices. What is man's rejection compared with the acceptance we have in Christ?

The impact we have on our world is in direct proportion to our being living sacrifices.

I'll never forget the time I was walking through a park when I saw a man in a wheelchair being unloaded from a van. I had just become convinced that God's healing was for today and not just for church people but for everybody as well. I remembered Jesus's evangelistic strategy: "Whatever city you enter, heal the sick." That plan would be just as effective today as it was when He spoke those words, if the church would just believe it. As I approached the man, a wave of fear came over me, and I panicked. Instead of stopping to ask him if he wanted prayer, I walked right by him. I made another lap around the park and walked past him again. Finally I thought that if I was going to make a difference in this world, I must overcome this fear and become that living sacrifice and reach out to this man in need. This man was a quadriplegic and was not able to speak. I asked his caretaker if I could pray for him, and she said yes.

When I told the man that I wanted to pray for him, he got a look in his eyes that has never left me. He had such gratitude; it was as if I was the only one who believed he could be set free from his body, which was more like a prison. I prayed and felt the presence of God surrounding us. After a few minutes, I stopped. I didn't see him get up, but I knew the Lord had touched him. My disappointment that he was not healed on the spot was tempered by the fact that I had just crossed into a new realm of living. I was now His. I could reach out to the most difficult cases, extend His love and power to those in need, and leave the results with Him.

Since that day I have seen many people healed. However, I do not see an instant manifestation of healing in most of the people for whom I pray. Often people I have prayed for will tell me that later that day or that week they experienced their healing. At one of our recent evangelistic outreaches, a woman came up to me and asked, "Do you

remember me?" I told her I didn't. She said she had come to our out-
reach the year before and that she had been paralyzed on her left side
by a stroke. She said I had prayed for her, and when she awoke the next
day, the paralysis was gone. Was it God's will to heal her? Of course.
Was it the right time? Of course. The only necessary ingredient was
my willingness to step out of my comfort zone and pray for her.

As long as I am willing to offer up my life as a living sacrifice, His
kingdom expands. We can reign with Him as long as we are willing
to lay down our lives for Him. I am a royal priest, and I reign when
the sacrifice is on the altar. People are looking for His kingdom to
be real, and the only way they see that kingdom is when they lose
themselves for that kingdom. Revelation 5:10 declares, "You have
made them to be a kingdom and priests to our God; and they shall
reign upon the earth." Many want to reign, but few want to sacrifice.
These two acts go hand in hand.

THE SACRIFICE OF PRAISE

The next area in which we fulfill our duty as royal priests is when
we offer up the sacrifice of praise. Hebrews 13:15 says, "Through
Him then, let us continually offer up a sacrifice of praise to God,
that is, the fruit of lips that give thanks to His name." The bat-
tleground in the Christian life is our minds. We have an enemy
who is warring with our new identity. Condemnation, shame, and
guilt are some of his most effective weapons to discourage us. He
is always accusing us of our failures or attacking the goodness of
God. One of the best remedies for these attacks is praising God.
We crush doubt and fear when we exalt His name and His word.
Satan's main strategy is separation. His goal in the garden was
man's separation from God and then separation from each other.

God is about reconciliation, and because we are now reconciled to our heavenly Father, let us continually praise Him.

When our circumstances contradict His goodness, sacrifices of praise are the hardest to make. Satan will always seize these opportunities to accuse God. You must not come into agreement with him and his lies that God does not care or have your best interest at heart. The sacrifice of praise will pull you back into agreement with God's innate goodness. Your challenge is to renew your minds and pull down any strongholds of thinking that would dethrone God. Remember our God is sovereign, and He is the only one who can bring good out of evil. Your praise will give you the right view of God. This, in turn, will increase your faith. It is much easier to receive from God when you have the correct view of Him. Clouded thinking about God results in a muted witness, and this prevents the kingdom of God from expanding.

The apostle Paul said the sacrifice of praise was in reality a safeguard for us. In Philippians 3:1 we read, "Finally brethren, rejoice in the Lord. To write the same things again is no trouble to me, and it is a safeguard for you." To the Thessalonians Paul charged, "Rejoice always." What kept the Israelites out of the Promised Land was their grumbling and complaining. Following their example will also cause us to forfeit our destiny. A heart of thanksgiving is a fertile field for faith to grow.

Crushing the "why" question is essential for the sacrifice of praise. Whenever we start to ask "Why me?" we open up ourselves to the trap of self-pity. Self-pity is an invitation to doubt God and opens us up to be offended. Offense then becomes a platform for unbelief, and we cease to reign. The "why" question is an assault on the sovereignty of God. Our sacrifice of praise reestablishes sovereignty and fuels our faith.

Graham Cooke, an amazing prophetic minister, made a brilliant observation when he said we must learn to live life relationally and not situationally. Living relationally means knowing that God is involved in every circumstance of life because He lives in us. Therefore, we should ask Him what He wants us to learn from each circumstance, trial, or disappointment. A better way of looking at life is to ask, "Father, what do you want me to know or how do you want to handle this issue?" To live situationally is to look at life apart from God. "How could this happen to me?" or "Why me?" is the language of separation. This is yet another invitation to embrace the orphan spirit. We feel abandoned and alone and cry out like Jesus's disciples when they said, "Lord, carest not that we perish?" Many Christians have echoed this familiar refrain through the centuries. Remember, God is in your boat. Gain His perspective of the storm in your life and begin to praise Him. We can reign through anything when we continually offer up the sacrifice of praise.

My wife and I often pray for our children. One season we were especially concerned for them. Usually my prayer was "Please, God, do something" or "Please help them." While listening to a teaching, I heard the teacher say, "If you are praying for your children, stop begging God to do something. Instead, bless God for what He is already doing in their life. Now, instead of praying fear-based prayers, release the sacrifice of praise and the spirit of faith for His guiding hand in your child's life." Within six months, we saw the answer to our prayers. During that time, my faith was in what God was doing, *not* in what my child was doing. Lift up the sacrifice of praise for your family. Keep an expectant eye for the prodigal to return. Your sovereign God has many ways to draw him or her back.

THE FINANCIAL SACRIFICE

The next area of dominion through sacrifice is our finances. Every time you and I willingly give to God from our finances, He honors the financial sacrifice. Too many of us live under the dominion of debt. God has a plan to provide abundance to all of His children if they will trust Him in this area. We all know what it's like to have too much month left at the end of the money. God is not indifferent to our needs. But as in every other area of the kingdom, the same eternal principle applies to money. What you sacrifice will return to you.

Sadly, this is a controversial area in the kingdom because of the abuse and misapplication of riches. We must never build a theology in reaction to error but only in response to truth. We must learn the truth about prosperity and the abundance that is part of our inheritance. One of the best ways to reveal God's will in this area is by reading 2 Corinthians 8 and 9. You will get a fresh revelation of the grace available to you in this area. Remember that dominion comes through sacrifice and that we must learn the keys to sacrificial giving if we want to prosper. God wants you to have an abundance to meet *every* good deed. Unfortunately, most Christians don't have an abundance to meet *any* good deed.

A key point to remember is that God is not after our money but after our hearts. When we give sacrificially, we shift our heart focus to God and His kingdom and not to things. Where your treasure is, your heart will also be. So the net result of giving to God is a renewed heart and access to His unlimited resources. We now become the cheerful givers that He desires and walk in the truth that it is better to give than receive. An old expression says that "if God can get it through you, He can get it to you." Become a river, not a reservoir of material blessings to others.

Seek God for your strategy for giving. Abraham, Isaac, and Jacob all had the same promise for provision. God revealed to each one of them that they were going to possess the land of Canaan. They each used a different strategy to secure that promise. Abraham gave one-tenth of his possessions to Melchizedek. Isaac sowed in time of famine. Jacob made a vow. Don't be held hostage to percentages of giving. Seek God for the amount you are to sacrifice each week, and he will reward you. Remember, He honors those who honor him with their wealth.

Another point to remember is that our confession must match our giving. Too many believers see little result from their sowing because of their negative confession about their financial condition. Leviticus 19:19 says, "You shall not sow your field with two kinds of seeds." Our negative confession is like seed killer on the financial seeds that we have just planted. Match your sacrificial giving with the sacrifice of praise. Believe God for your provision and confess that His promises are true and that He will bless you. Don't let fear and negative confessions rob you of your inheritance.

CHAPTER 7

WHO OWNS YOU?

THREE WORDS CHANGED MY LIFE. Three words opened the door. Three words became my passport to victory. The Lord simply asked me, "Who owns you?" This was not the answer I was not looking for. I was in the middle of asking the Lord about a difficult situation when He asked me this question. I find it a fascinating dynamic that when we seek the Lord on one level, He often answers us from a completely different level. That question about ownership led me to 1 Corinthians 7:23: "You were bought with a price; do not become slaves of men." The obvious answer is that the Lord owns me. Why then should I let other people or circumstances own me?

My mind began to rebel at the simplicity of His question. Lord, do you have any idea how difficult that person is? Do you see how frustrating this job is? Each time I sensed the gentle voice of the Spirit saying to me, "Why do you let them own you when I own you?" It wasn't "what" He was saying to me; it was the "how" that troubled me. I knew He was presenting me with a doorway to freedom, but I couldn't find the handle. How could I live a life free from people and circumstances? Was I supposed to live in denial or just grit my teeth at every inconvenience? Let's be honest; people do irritate us. Unpleasant things happen. Wouldn't it be easier to just pray these people away so they wouldn't cross our path?

One day I pulled up in front of a Kmart, and I happened to get the parking space closest to the front door. At the same time, I noticed that my van was the identical make and color as the van next to me. A man about my age was sitting in the driver's seat. As I was about to get out of my van, I saw a woman coming out of the store heading directly toward me. In a flash I knew she thought my van was her van. She was also in a full rage and was yelling something I couldn't understand. Assuming my van was her van, she pulled open the passenger door of my van still yelling. When she realized the mistake, she quickly went from fury to nervous laughter and apology. I glanced over at her husband, who, knowing full well he had just dodged a bullet, was laughing his head off. At that moment, I saw something that helped me process my dilemma with ownership. This woman had exercised a choice to go from rage to laughter in a split second. Instead of surrendering to her emotions, she controlled them. She was able to make the switch because of the external challenge of finding me in the car instead of her husband. Could I make the same switch with some internal challenge?

After a few days of praying about what to do, my internal challenge was to say to myself, "You don't own me," to everyone who pushed my buttons. Standing in the checkout line in Walmart, when an employee seemed to go to China for a price check, I would internally declare, "This does not own me." I began to practice this discipline daily. Until I began doing this, I had no idea of how much of a slave I was. I realized that, previously, I had been signing up for chains daily. I began to ask the Lord for further insight into this challenge of ownership.

The Lord began to highlight my preoccupation with justice. The fact that we live in an unjust world is not news. Injustice is real and needs to be addressed, but the Lord wanted to show me something deeper with regard to the way I processed life. From the moment we can walk and talk, we are quite aware of what is fair or unfair. For many children the first words out of their mouths after "mom" and "dad" are "that's not fair." They are like little lawyers running around in diapers declaring what is just or unjust. "Objection, Your Honor!" follows most commands. "Eat your peas" is followed by, "That's not fair." "Go to bed" is followed by, "That's not fair." "Pick up your toys" is followed by, "That's not fair." You get the picture.

Choosing Freedom over Justice

We fine-tune our sense of justice all our lives. Sibling rivalries, insults from friends, and humiliations at the hands of a teacher or the neighborhood bully all inflame our need for justice. Much of our counseling surrounds the wounds we suffer from an unjust world.

The trap we fall into is choosing justice over freedom. Jesus demonstrated how to live this kind of life. "For you have been called for this purpose, since Christ suffered for you, leaving you an *example* for you to follow in His steps, WHO COMMITTED NO SIN, NOR WAS ANY DECEIT FOUND IN HIS MOUTH; and while being reviled, He did not revile in return; while suffering, He uttered no threats, but kept entrusting Himself to Him who judges righteously" (1 Pet. 2:21–23, italics mine).

Jesus did not let anything or anyone own Him. His trial was grossly unfair. The physical and verbal abuse He endured was terrific. But Jesus was able to entrust justice to His Father. The Pharisees did not own Him. Pilate and the Roman soldiers did not own Him. These revelations challenged me to live the same way. Could I take every inconvenience, every offense, and every slight and quickly declare to myself that they would not own me? Could I, like Jesus, commit the justice that is due me to my heavenly Father while living in an unjust world? Could freedom increase and justice decrease if I incorporated this internal filter into the way I processed life?

Let us take a deeper look at Jesus before Pilate. Most people standing before a Roman governor would be trembling, but not Jesus. Pilate saw that someone greater than Rome was before him. He understood this, and it scared him. When Pilate threatened him with death, Jesus bluntly told the governor he had no authority over Him. What a statement! The kingdom of God was on full display. Pilate could see the confidence that Jesus carried and tried even harder to release Him. Eventually he turned Jesus over to the wishes of the Jews and had Him crucified.

The world is watching how we process life. Can we follow His example? If we refuse to empower people and circumstances in our lives, then our witness will improve dramatically.

In the Sermon on the Mount, Jesus mentions three incidents highlighting the need to choose freedom over justice. In the first incident, he declares, "But I say to you, do not resist an evil person; but whoever slaps you on your right cheek, turn the other to him also" (Matt. 5:39). "Turning the other cheek" has for centuries been one of the hallmark characteristics of true Christianity. This one phrase implies that we are connected to a greater reality that transcends the value systems of earth. Overcoming evil with good is now the standard by which we are to live. It is a powerful proclamation of the gospel. Jesus astounded the world by making this statement because it was so contrary to our fallen nature. But how often do we turn the other cheek?

The second incident invites this challenge: "If anyone wants to sue you and take your shirt, let him have your coat also" (Matt. 5:40). We live in a very litigious country. We have more lawyers per capita than any other country. Suing people is big business. Can you imagine being sued and then offering the person who sued you even more than he or she asked? Jesus was not some wild-eyed idealist. He knew that to demonstrate His kingdom we would have to live a life contrary to the prevailing values of man. It was the lifestyle He chose to live and invited us to follow.

The third incident was particularly offensive to the Jews of Jesus's day. The following advice sums it up: "Whoever forces you to go one mile, go with him two" (Matt. 5:41). Roman soldiers could command any Jew to carry their bundles for one mile. Rome had conquered Israel and was the occupying force. Jesus now demonstrated how they could conquer Rome with a kingdom lifestyle. Go the second mile with a smile and a spring in your step. You demonstrate that Rome does not own you but that Almighty God does. Only God can give you the grace to go the second mile.

After the incident at Kmart, I had insight into these verses that I never had before. In each instance of injustice that Jesus mentions, we are to choose freedom over justice. We show the world that we are connected to a higher power of life by this choice. We are not part of this world. We are citizens of the kingdom of God. For His kingdom to manifest on earth as it is in heaven, we must demonstrate the freedom that the kingdom of God offers.

Another area of deep influence in our lives is our families. Many of us are under the pressure to live up to their expectations. In this area, knowing who truly owns you will help you live free from their controlling interests. Although we honor our mother and father, we all should eventually come to the place of honoring our heavenly Father above everyone else. When Jesus's mother and brothers wanted to seize Him and bring Him home because they thought He had lost His senses (Mark 3:21; Matt. 12:46–50), Jesus asked this pertinent question: "Who are my mother and my brothers?" He answered this question by saying, "For whoever does the will of my

Father who is in heaven, he is my brother and sister and mother." This principle applies to any human relationship that would try to control you.

The Power of Forgiveness

One of the major foundation blocks of our Christian life is forgiveness. As people who have been forgiven much, we are challenged to forgive those who have hurt us. For many, forgiving almost seems like an injustice. Forgiving our enemies can be perceived as giving a free pass to someone who has wrecked our lives. The truth is that when we refuse to forgive, we still empower those people to continue to hurt us. How many of us replay old conversations and incidents that wounded us many years ago? And every time we revisit these incidents in our minds, the pain is just as real as when it first happened.

Jesus said that unforgiveness is like being put in jail. The moment we choose to forgive and let mercy triumph over justice, we experience a profound sense of freedom. Those who wounded us no longer own us.

Finding the Inner Strength to Overcome

Another example the Lord highlighted for me on how to overcome injustice is found in Hebrews 10:32–34:

> But remember the former days, when after being enlightened, you endured a great conflict of sufferings, partly by being made a public spectacle through reproaches and tribulations, and partly by becoming sharers with those who were so treated. For you showed sympathy to the prisoners, and accepted

joyfully the seizure of your property knowing that you have for yourselves a better possession and an abiding one.

Here, a group of believers refused to be owned by adverse circumstances. Whom do you know who would rejoice if his or her house was confiscated? Being made into a public spectacle was apparently no sweat for the people in this crowd. We read about these events, yet we never seek to incorporate this lifestyle into our own. These dear saints learned the truth: that our lives are defined by heaven, not earth. "A better possession and an abiding one" is the key to letting heaven define your life. If you let earth define you, then you will be a slave to whatever unpleasant circumstance you are experiencing.

Our true DNA is that of an overcomer. As 1 John 5:4 says, "For whatever is born of God overcomes the world; and this is the victory that overcomes the world—our faith." Faith rooted in our true identity amplifying that we are citizens of another realm. Listening to many Christians speak, you would think that overcoming is the exception, not the rule. Life dominates them, not the other way around. The Bible states that I am seated with Christ in heavenly places. From this vantage point, we should be looking down on our circumstances, not looking up at them. We overcome from a heavenly perspective. We are seated with Him, welded to His love, and knowing that "if God be for us, who can be against us?" (Rom. 8:31).

Why should I let someone's lack of grace change my standing in grace? Why should it matter what people say about me when I know what God says about me? If I am accepted in the beloved, why should man's rejection matter? We have elevated people and circumstances to define and validate us when God already validates us as sons and daughters and heirs of God. When you are free from self, then and only then are you free from others. The more you center your thinking on yourself, the more you become a victim. You have been redeemed. Your life is now owned by the one who created you. His ownership is your ticket to freedom.

The apostle Paul states, "For I am trained in the secret of overcoming all things" (Phil. 4:11 TPT). In other translations of this verse, Paul says he learned to be content in all circumstances. The word "content" means to have the inner strength to overcome. It implies that you are not controlled by outward events. Where does this strength come from? Paul goes on to say, "I can do all things through Christ who strengthens me." The context here is not the strength to do something but the inner strength to overcome something. Paul is saying that we can be the same no matter what circumstance we find ourselves in.

Paul was not an idle proclaimer of this truth. He lived his life without letting anything or anyone own him. The best evidence of this is found in Acts 16, when he and Silas were imprisoned in Philippi. With their backs beaten raw and with their feet locked in stocks, they began to sing. It was not a chorus of complaint but a celebration of praise to God. Two innocent men, unjustly accused, imprisoned, and beaten, chose freedom. They refused to let the situation own then. Instead, they owned the situation. Paul and Silas modeled freedom while in prison. What happened next was truly amazing. A great earthquake shook the prison to its foundation, the prison's doors flung open, and the prisoners' chains fell off. I believe that earthquake was heaven's applause to their praise.

In a similar vein, when we stand firm and refuse to permit circumstances to own us, our examples will inspire people who are prisoners to their circumstances. They will be empowered to walk out of their prison cells and let the chains of injustice fall from their hands. By not letting anyone own us, we will send shock waves of freedom to those watching and listening to us. Example is still the most powerful witness.

CHAPTER 8

COVENANT PEOPLE

I BELIEVE ONE OF THE least understood truths in the body of Christ is covenant. We all know the difference between the old covenant and the new covenant. We may even know the difference between the covenant of law and the covenant of grace. But the essential power of covenant is lost in our modern era. We are more familiar with contracts. In a typical contract, each party spells out his or her respective responsibilities. In contrast, a covenant is an ironclad commitment between two bodies that never changes. Marriage is technically a covenant between two people who agree to love, honor, and cherish each other until death. Unfortunately, with the divorce rate so high, we see the covenant of marriage as just another contract that can be broken.

My wife, Beth, and I were married in Spain in 1980 while we were working as missionaries. Before our marriage, we were informed that there was no divorce in Spain. As far as the Spanish government was concerned, when you said, "I do," you agreed that only death would break this covenant. It was amazing living in a country, where the view of the permanency of marriage was higher than in most Christian churches. Since then the marriage laws in Spain have changed, but it was quite sobering to enter into a relationship that was a true covenant.

Understanding the power of covenant is the basis for living a confident Christian life. Our faith must be anchored in the conviction that God has made an eternal agreement with us that cannot be broken. We are all familiar with warranties. Companies offer warranties on their products to show the public that they are committed to the quality and the performance of their products. Craftsman tools became the most trusted brand in this country because Sears offered a lifetime guarantee on its products. You could own a wrench for thirty years, and if it broke, you could take it back to Sears and get a brand-new wrench, no questions asked. Warranties produce confidence. Covenants were established by God to man to achieve the same purpose.

The first blood covenant recorded in the Bible is found in Genesis 15:7–21. God takes Abraham out, shows him the stars in the sky, and declares, "So shall your descendants be." Abraham believes God, and his profession of faith is counted to him as righteousness. In the very next verse, God says He is also going to give all the land of Canaan to Abraham and his descendants, to which Abraham replies, "How may I know that I shall possess it?" I marveled when I first saw this. How could Abraham, the father of faith, move from faith to unbelief so quickly? He believes God for millions of people but has no faith for God to house them in their own land. All we have to do is look at our own lives to understand this dynamic. All of us have faith in some promise of God but are paralyzed by unbelief in some other promise. Knowing this, God instituted a blood covenant to guarantee His promise of blessing to Abraham.

In ancient days covenants were performed when two parties or nations came together to form an alliance. They would take certain animals and cut then in two. They would make a pathway between the severed parts. Then each party would walk between the severed parts and state the terms and conditions of the covenant. They would also declare that they would die like these animals if they broke the covenant. This is known as a conditional covenant. Each party has certain responsibilities that must be fulfilled for the covenant to be maintained.

The law instituted by Moses was a conditional covenant. In Exodus 24:1–8, when Moses reads the law to the people of Israel, they declare, "All that the Lord has spoken we will do!" The people are affirming their part in holding up this covenant. Moses then commands a sacrifice be made and the blood sprinkled on the altar and the people. The sad truth of this conditional covenant was that the nation of Israel did not live up to its terms of the covenant. The Israelites often turned their backs on God and worshiped other gods. Because they broke the covenant, the Lord sent judgment to the nation until the people repented and renewed their devotion to follow Him.

It is important to understand the reason why the covenant God made with Abraham is better than the covenant He made with Moses. Abraham's covenant was an unconditional covenant. When Abraham split the animals in two, God alone, in the form of a burning oven and a flaming torch, passed through the separated animals. God alone would fulfill the terms of this agreement. Abraham's only responsibility in this unconditional covenant was to believe the guaranteed promise of God. The apostle Paul further clarifies this point in his letter to the Galatians. Let's look at a few translations to deepen our understanding:

- **Galatians 3:20 (NASB):** "Now a mediator is not for one party only; whereas God is only one."
- **Galatians 3:20 (AMP):** "Now a go-between (intermediary) has to do with *and* implies more than one party [there can be no mediator with just one person]. Yet God is [only] one

Person [and He was the sole party in giving the promise to Abraham]. But the Law was a contract between two, God and Israel; its validity was dependent on both."

* **Galatians 3:19–20 (Message):** "Obviously this law was not a firsthand encounter with God. It was arranged by angelic messengers through a middleman, Moses. But if there is a middleman as there was at Sinai, then the people are not dealing directly with God, are they? But the original promise is the direct blessings of God, received by faith."

In W. E. Vine's *Expository Dictionary of New Testament Words* (1966, 54), he defines the word "mediator" found in Galatians 3:19–20. "Here the contrast is between the promise given to Abraham and the giving of the Law. The Law was a covenant enacted between God and the Jewish people requiring fulfillment by both parties. But with the promise to Abraham ALL the obligations were assumed by God, which is implied in the statement 'But God is one.'"

Here again we see the superiority of the new covenant. God alone guarantees the terms of the contract. This is the essence of grace. Grace is what saves us, and grace is what keeps us. We only have to believe.

Whenever our faith is weak, we must focus on the covenant we have with God to strengthen our belief in His promises. Remember, the blood of Jesus Christ guarantees our covenant. The Last Supper was really a covenant meal during which Jesus said, "This cup which is poured out for you is the new covenant in my blood." Jesus is the guarantor of a better covenant enacted with better promises because He sealed the covenant with His own blood. Like Abraham, we are only required to believe.

To further expand our understanding and appreciation of covenant, I want us to look at Hebrews 6:11–18:

And we desire that each of you show the same diligence so as to realize the full assurance of hope until the end, so that you will not be sluggish, but imitators of those who through faith and patience inherit the promises. For when God made the promise to Abraham, since He could swear by no one greater, He swore by Himself saying, "I WILL SURELY BLESS YOU AND MULTIPLY YOU." And so, having patiently waited, he obtained the promise. For men swear by one greater than themselves, and with them an oath is given as confirmation is an end of every dispute. In the same way God, desiring even more to show the heirs of the promise the unchangeableness of His purpose, *interposed with an oath*, so that by two unchangeable things in which it is impossible for God to lie, we who have taken refuge would have strong encouragement to take hold of the hope that is set before us. (Emphasis mine.)

Pay attention to the words "interposed with an oath." Most of us are unaware that this is the language of covenant. The word "interposed" is better translated as "guarantee." The "oath" spoken here is a reference to the blood covenant that God made with Abraham. We see this connection in Luke 1:72–72: "And to remember His holy *covenant*, the *oath* which He swore to Abraham our father" (emphasis mine). Thus, "interposed with an oath" could be rendered as "He guaranteed it with a covenant." There is no higher guarantee than God's covenant commitment.

I believe these few verses in Hebrews are the Christian "Magna Carta" of faith. Instituted in England in 1215, the Magna Carta guaranteed the rights of the people under King John. From this document evolved constitutional government, and it served as a model for future democracies. These few verses are the basis of our confident access to all the promises of God.

What the writer of Hebrews reveals is the heart of God who "desires even more" to show to each one of His children the depths He went to secure his or her inheritance. The first thing we must see is the intense love of our God in His relation to us. Isaiah 55:3 gives us a preview of our new confident standing before God: "And I will make an everlasting covenant with you, according to the faithful mercies shown to David." God's covenant is rooted in love. The words "faithful mercies" are rooted in the Hebrew word *hesed*, which is often translated as "mercy." We normally think of mercy as God overlooking our sins and the punishment that goes with that sin. But mercy can also mean a deep, loyal love. David ended Psalm 23 by saying, "Surely goodness and mercy will follow me all the days of my life." The word "mercy" here is better translated as "loving kindness," which implies a deep sense of loyalty. So we can read the final verse of Psalm 23 as "Surely goodness and deep, loyal love will follow me all the days of my life."

When I first saw the depth of the meaning of the word *hesed*, I felt the Lord speak to me that this was a "now" word for His church. If we are to be rooted and grounded in love, we must meditate on the deep implications of that loyal love.

Here is a more colorful definition of the word *hesed*: "the consistent, ever-faithful, relentless, constantly pursuing, lavish, extravagant, unrestrained, furious love of God the Father for you." Wash your face with these words. Let them refresh your spirit and renew your passion for the one who loves you with an everlasting loyal love.

The favorable year of the Lord is rooted in covenant and loyal love. You cannot be confident in accessing to your identity and your inheritance without understanding the commitment that God has provided for His children.

CHAPTER 9

THREE CHEERS FOR THE ZELOPHEHAD GIRLS

Zelophehad had five amazing daughters: There was Mahlah, Noah, Hoglah, Milcah, and Tirzah. When it comes to pursuing God for uncharted blessings, these women reign supreme. By unchartered blessings, I mean blessings that are consistent with God's character but not explicitly spelled out. These women serve as role models for all who want God's best and refuse to take no for an answer. If we are going to access our inheritance, we must pay close attention to the example left by these women. Their story is found in Numbers 27:1–8:

> Then the daughters of Zelophehad, the son of Hepher, the son of Machir, the son of Manasseh, of the families of Manasseh the son of Joseph, came near; and these are the names of his daughters: Mahlah, Noah and Hoglah and Milcah and Tirzah. They stood before Moses and before Eleazar the priest and before the leaders and all the congregation, at the doorway of the tent of meeting, saying, "Our father died in the wilderness, yet he was not among the company of those who gathered themselves together against the Lord in the

company of Korah, but he died in his own sin, and he had no sons. Why should the name of our father be withdrawn from among his family because he had no son? Give us a possession among our father's brothers." So Moses brought their case before the Lord. Then the Lord spoke to Moses, saying, "The daughters of Zelophehad are right in their statements. You shall surely give them a hereditary possession among their father's brothers, and you shall transfer the inheritance to their father to them. Further, you shall speak to the sons of Israel, saying, 'If a man dies and has no son, then you shall transfer his inheritance to his daughter.'"

For people to bring disputes to Moses was not uncommon, but usually men stood before him. This culture was male-dominated, and the laws of inheritances normally favored sons. I can only imagine the courage that it took for these women to approach Moses. He was the great lawgiver. He was the one who went toe-to-toe with Pharaoh and won, who lifted up his staff and parted the Red Sea. He was on the mountain of God for forty days when the nation of Israel trembled. There was great thunder on that mountain, with flashes of lightning and loud trumpet blasts. Moses's face shone with the glory of God in such a way that no one could look at him. This was the arena the women entered to make their request.

God told Moses to take a census of the sons of the tribes of Israel and grant each tribe and family their portion in the Promised Land. As far as these women were concerned, there was a glaring problem: they had been excluded from the inheritance of the land. These women were challenging the laws in a direct dispute with Moses and an indirect conflict to God.

The Promised Land was no small promise to the nation of Israel. It was the ultimate promise. These women had all heard the stories of Abraham being promised this land. The first blood covenant recorded between God and Abraham was to guarantee the land that God had promised. Isaac and Jacob all held on to the same promise. I'm sure during the Israelites' four hundred years in Egypt, this promise was repeated to every generation. One can only imagine the excitement when the Israelites came to the border of the Promised Land at Kadesh-Barnea. Twelve spies were sent in, and they came back declaring, "This surely is a land flowing with milk and honey." And then tragedy struck. Ten of the spies gave a bad report: along with amazing fruits, giants and fortified cities awaited them. This discouraged the Israelites from taking the long-awaited promise. Instead of seizing this glorious moment to go in, the Israelites rebelled and spent forty years in the wilderness. God's judgment was that all the males who refused to go in would die in the wilderness and that only their children would occupy the land. Zelophehad had refused to go, and he died in the wilderness, leaving his five daughters to go into the land.

Dreams die hard. And these women were not about to let their dream of having an inheritance in the Promised Land die with their father. I wonder how many days and how many conversations took place before these women gathered the courage to confront Moses about the injustice of the situation. Most people take no for an answer. Many listen to the dream killers they meet—those who rob them of their destiny. In the space of a few minutes, the ten spies had put to death the dreams of a whole nation. Somehow, these women refused to believe that God would let that happen. No matter how unprecedented their request might have seemed, they wanted the dream that God had placed into their hearts to manifest.

Many of us have dreams and desires that seem fantastic to believe. Could God actually use us or fulfill these deep longings? Don't dismiss these inner dreams. The daughters of Zelophehad changed the laws of an entire nation because they refused to let their dreams die. I sometimes wonder if God is looking for people who have that inner conviction—that boldness that will not let them rest until they see Him honor His word. I think of Mary at the wedding feast of Cana. She jump-started Jesus's ministry because she put a demand on the anointing that was within Him. "Not now" and "not this time" will not deter God's adventurers. Can you push beyond these negative barriers to see your dreams come true? Try to induce labor to give birth to every prophetic word, every dream, and every desire that God has placed within you.

I wonder what the atmosphere was like after they spoke to Moses and he went in to inquire of the Lord. Were the men annoyed that they had dared to breach convention and ask for something so unthinkable? I think the Lord was secretly pleased because He found some women who were more passionate about His promise than the vast majority of the men of Israel.

Faith always pleases God! Unbelief is always a vote for you; faith is a vote for God. If nothing is impossible with God, then we should live a life without limits. If God can do exceedingly above and beyond all that we can ask or think, why do we think and ask for such mundane things, such as for help with the rent, with a car payment, and so on? I think Moses was pleasantly surprised by God's reaction. God, indeed, sided with the daughters' request. If there is a book in you, write it. If there is a movie in you, shoot it. If there is a song in you, sing it. If there is a business idea burning inside you, then start the business. We have to be relentless to claim our share of the Promised Land.

Moses is the patron saint for changing God's mind. How many times did Moses intercede for the nation of Israel when God wanted to wipe it out? Moses even had God agree to remain with him and his followers on their journey by promising that "his presence would go with them" (Exod. 33:1–17). These women were kindred spirits.

Soon Moses emerged from the tent of meeting and declared that God had agreed with the Zelophehad women. They would get their share of the inheritance in the Promised Land. The impossible had just become possible. Boldness and faith had resurrected their stillborn dream. I truly believe God delights in His children wrestling with Him about their futures. "Call to me and I will answer you and I will tell you great and mighty things that you don't know" (Jer. 33:3): this is our ready invitation to ask outside the box. What would you attempt to do if money were no object? God has all the resources you need. Start dreaming with God. Put your name on the list of those who have attempted great things for the kingdom of God. Leave timidity behind. Launch out from the secure shores of mediocrity and sail into your destiny.

Once God gives us the green light for our dreams, a very important ingredient is needed: patience. By faith and patience, we will inherit the promises. After the Zelophehad girls had completed their victory lap, they came to terms with the fact that they still were not in the Promised Land. It would take another twenty-five years before God's judgment would be fulfilled and they could enter the Promised Land. I once heard someone say that if you are willing to stand forever, you won't have to stand long. Never let go of your dreams. Remember, you will only be stopped by surrendering to what discourages you or what offends you. Refuse to give in to discouragement and offense, and live a life of possibilities.

Another challenge rose up before Zelophehad's daughters. Moses died. Would Joshua still honor the request that Moses had granted them? (Josh. 17:3–4). You can imagine how the enemy probably attacked them at this moment. We all know how hard it is to continue to believe in a promise when the circumstances seem to move in the opposite direction. I'm sure that fear and doubt must have risen in them, trying to steal their dream. But pushing aside the fear and doubt, these courageous women boldly stood before Joshua and Eleazar to secure the promise that Moses had made to them. Joshua honored their request and secured their inheritance. The lapse of time and the change of leadership did not discourage these women. We often celebrate the spirit that was on Joshua and Caleb, but rarely do we celebrate these remarkable women. Let them be an inspiration to all who have no plan B.

The Lord has given me an amazing promise for my ministry. Over the years I have repeatedly written that prophecy on the flyleaf of my Bible. After waiting thirty years, I stopped writing that promise. One day while reading the Psalms, I came to this line: "Remember the word to your servant, in which you have made me hope" (Ps. 119:49). I felt the Lord telling me to revive this promise and to start writing it again in my Bible. He then instructed me to confess this promise aloud. We don't have to remind God because He is forgetful, but we have to remind ourselves of His faithfulness to honor His word. Through faith and patience, we inherit the promises. Shortly after this happened, my ministry changed. Fresh impartations and fresh revelations revitalized my ministry and me. We must steward the words that God has spoken to us. I have yet to realize the fullness of God's word to me, but I refuse to settle for anything less than His best.

CHAPTER 10

GILGAL, ANYONE?

I BECAME A CHRISTIAN IN 1976, and like many new Christians, I knew more about the New Testament than the Old Testament. My focus was on Jesus in the gospels and the exploits of the early church in the book of Acts. One day while I was visiting a Christian bookstore, an older man who worked there came up to me and asked what books of the Old Testament I was reading. I replied that I never read the Old Testament because the New Testament was more interesting. He made a statement to me that I will never forget: "The Old Testament is the New Testament contained, and the New Testament is the Old Testament explained." I wasn't sure what he meant, but it intrigued me to find how the New Testament was hiding among the books of the Old Testament and how the Old was explained in the New Testament. Here's an example of this truth.

Before the nation of Israel could conquer the Promised Land, God had to give the Israelites an identity upgrade. For forty years in the wilderness and four hundred years before that, their identity was that of slaves. Even though God had miraculously delivered them from Pharaoh and his army, they still saw themselves as powerless slaves. This was evident when they rejected the challenge to take the Promised Land that had just been spied out. "We were like grasshoppers" was their estimation of their identity. Having a misplaced identity will always thwart you from apprehending your destiny.

In Joshua 5:9 we read that the Lord said to Joshua, "This day I have rolled away the reproach of Egypt from you." So the name of that place is called Gilgal to this day. The name Gilgal means "to roll way or remove." Circumcision was the method by which God removed the Israelites' shame as slaves.

Circumcision was the original identifier for God's people. The practice was given by God to Abraham to symbolize that they were His covenant people, belonging to Him alone. Moses received his commission from God to return to Egypt to deliver the nation of Israel. Along the way he was instructed to circumcise his son. Then, in an amazing incident recorded in Exodus 4:24–26, God sought to put Moses to death. The issue was circumcision. Apparently, for the forty years Moses lived in Midian, he did not continue the practice of circumcision. He must have been gravely ill or too incapacitated to perform it himself so Moses's wife, Zipporah, performed the circumcision on his son. Circumcision was a sign to validate the Israelites as God's chosen people. Circumcision also harkened back to the covenant in which God had promised the land to Israel (Gen. 17:1–14). How could Moses return to Egypt without the physical testimony being on the body of his own son? The whole purpose of God sending Moses to Egypt was to deliver the Jews from Pharaoh and then bring them into the land of promise.

When Israel rebelled at taking the land, the Lord pronounced judgment on them. "According to the number of days which you spied out the land, forty days, for every day you shall bear your guilt for a year, even forty years, and you will know my opposition" (Num. 14:34). The covenant seemed to be suspended during this time of judgment. No one was circumcised. No ongoing ceremony confirmed the covenant God had made with Abraham. No outward sign signified their unique identity as God's people and their unique inheritance of the Promised Land.

God took Israel out of Egypt, but He could not get Egypt out of Israel. How many times did Israelites complain, saying, "Take us back to Egypt," "We want the cucumbers and the melons and the leeks and the garlic of Egypt," and, finally, "Is it because there were no graves in Egypt that you have taken us away to die in the wilderness?" Their continual focus was on their past identity. Too many of us still focus on the fact that we are sinners and not saints and thus have a hard time accessing our destiny.

We often talk about salvation by faith alone. Salvation is more than just being born again and being qualified for eternal life. The real challenge is to live by faith each day in the new identity that we have been given by Christ. From identity comes security in our relationship with God. From that place of security, we can lay hold of our promised land. The promised land for the believer is all the promises found in God's word. From this place we can change the world. We can invade the earth as the people of God who have all of heaven's resources available to them. We begin to pray with renewed confidence. We pray from heaven to earth, not earth to heaven. By this I mean we pray the promise, not the problem. Our prayers are now based on the promises of God that are rooted in covenant. We are not begging God as if we were orphans. We are the sons and daughters who understand our true standing before God and who are confident that all of God's promises to us are yes and amen.

For us Christians, our Gilgal moment is when we were circumcised by Christ. In this act, our old identity as sinners and slaves to sin are cut away, as Colossians 2:11–14 makes clear:

And in Him you were also circumcised with a circumcision made without hands, in the removal of the body of the flesh by the circumcision of Christ; having been buried with Him in baptism, in which you were also raised up with Him through faith in the working of God, who raised Him from the dead. When you were dead in your transgressions and the uncircumcision of your flesh, He made you alive together with Him, having forgiven us all our transgressions, having canceled out the certificate of debt consisting of decrees against us, which was hostile to us; and He has taken it out of the way, having nailed it to the cross.

The reproach of Egypt was the shame of being a slave and subservient to Pharaoh. For Christians, our reproach and shame was our identity before we met Christ. We were sinners by nature and slaves to sin. We were the sons of disobedience held captive by Satan to do his will. Christ came to change that reality.

The way Pharaoh pursued Israel to get them back into slavery is the same way Satan pursues us. Now that we know Christ, Satan still wants to blind our minds from our true redeemed identity. The enemy of our souls seeks to have us live our lives in the wilderness of a limited Christian experience. Christians who do not know how to access their promised land are no threat to the kingdom of darkness. To counter attack these assaults, our faith must be grounded in the work Christ did on our behalf. He cut away the body of flesh and broke the power of sin. Sin's power is in the law, and Christ abolished the law, having "nailed it to the cross."(Col. 2:14) Now we can stand before God without any sense of shame. We are now washed. We are now sanctified. We are now justified in the name of our Lord Jesus Christ (1 Cor. 6:11). Through the abundance of grace and the gift of righteousness, we will reign as kings in life (Rom. 5:17, AMP).

Knowing these truths will give us great confidence to take our promised land. No longer will we question our standing before God. Not only will we boldly approach the throne of grace but we will boldly pursue the destiny God has designed for us. We are heirs of God and joint heirs of His son, Jesus Christ. All the resources of heaven are now available to His people. Whatever He has is now yours. The works that He did are now available to all who believe.

The church must do a better job of rolling away the shame of our previous identity. In our preaching and teaching, we must strive for that Gilgal moment when we present to the body of Christ a clear pathway to shame-free living. If we are holy and blameless and beyond reproach, then let us say so with conviction and clarity. We must end the confusion of proclaiming a mixed identity of saint and sinner.

One way to know if you have not reached your Gilgal moment is if you still see yourself as a sinner. You may even be quick to look for scriptures that confirm your old identity as a sinner. If this is so, then the reproach of Egypt is still on you. Many Christians fail in this understanding because they somehow think that if they cease declaring themselves sinners, then they will deny the reality that they do occasionally sin. Remember our sin nature was circumcised. If we sin, it is because we choose to sin, not because we are slaves to sin. A better approach is to search for and meditate on those scriptures that confirm that you are a saint. Faith in your true, righteous standing before God, will roll away any vestiges of shame that you are a sinner. Finally you will arrive at Gilgal.

CHAPTER 11

TEN TIMES BETTER

WHEN DANIEL WAS LED INTO exile along with the captives from Israel, he was chosen with some other young men to serve in King Nebuchadnezzar's court. He was offered the finest food and drink from the king's table. Being a Jew, Daniel refused because he did not want to defile himself. The overseer was alarmed by his behavior and said Daniel could lose his head if he refused the king's delicacies. Daniel made a deal with the overseer and said that he and his friends would only eat vegetables and drink water for ten days. After ten days he could compare Daniel's and his friends' appearances to those of the other candidates. At the end of ten days, Daniel and his friends appeared better and fatter than the other young men. Because Daniel refused to compromise his true identity, the king found him and his friends ten times better than all the other magicians and astrologers in his kingdom (Dan. 1:1–17).

Many elements define who we are. When a couple finds out that they are going to have a baby, the first thing they want to know is if the baby is a boy or a girl. Gender is our first point of identification. The next level of identification is race. This is followed by nationality. Another point that defines us is our religious affiliation. As we grow older, more and more levels of identification are added. Your educational background and your occupation are also key identifiers.

Our political identity is huge in our country, which is now so polarized. Each one of us has a host of items that define us, from sports to fashion and music, to name just a few.

When I was growing up, the fact that I was Irish and Catholic clearly marked me. These two points seemed to supersede all other points of identification. When President John F. Kennedy was running for president, our parish was excited by the fact that America might elect the first Catholic for president. The fact that he was Irish added even more to his appeal. There was one problem, though: my father did not like him and wasn't going to vote for him. I remember the nuns in school coming up to me and saying, "Is it true your father is not voting for Kennedy? Doesn't he know that he is one of *us*?" Because I was only ten years old, I didn't know what to say. I only knew that my dad had flunked tribal loyalty.

"One of us" is the password to most loyalties. Being part of our gang, our neighborhood, or our school contains all the earmarks that identify us as being "one of us." Unfortunately, many of these parochial loyalties surpass our Christian loyalty. Jesus even said that loyalty to him might get us killed. Jesus even raised the bar regarding loyalty to Him when He said that anyone who loves his or her father or mother more than Him is not worthy to be His disciple.

In a world separated by so many customs and loyalties, Jesus came to make "one new man." In this way, all our differences would be rolled up in our identity in Christ. This identity would surpass all other identities. Consider how the apostle Paul describes this in Ephesians 2:11–19:

> Therefore remember, that formerly you, the Gentiles in the flesh, who are called "Uncircumcision" which is performed in the flesh by human hands—remember that you were at that time separate from Christ, excluded from the commonwealth

of Israel, and strangers to the covenants of promise, having no hope and without God in the world. But now in Christ Jesus you who formally were far off have been brought near by the blood of Christ. For He Himself is our peace, who made both groups into one and broke down the barrier of the dividing wall, by abolishing in His flesh the enmity, which is the law of commandments contained in ordinances, so that in Himself He might make one new man, thus establishing peace, and might reconcile them both in one body to God through the cross, by having put to death the enmity. AND HE CAME AND PREACHED PEACE TO YOU WHO WERE FAR AWAY, AND PEACE TO THOSE WHO WERE NEAR; FOR THROUGH Him we both have our access in one Spirit to the Father. So then you are no longer strangers and aliens, but you are fellow citizens with the saints, and are of God's household.

To the Jews, loyalty to their ethnic and religious identity was everything. They could not conceive of embracing any other nation or religion outside of their own. Their past tragedies were rooted in their intermingling with other nations and their gods. As bad as the Pharisees were in Jesus's day, they kept the nation in check against the backsliding and compromising that marked their past. The destruction of Solomon's temple and the Assyrian and Babylonian captivities were vivid historical reminders of the penalty of wavering in their loyalty to the God of Abraham, Isaac, and Jacob. But God had a bigger plan than they could imagine. God said to Abraham that all the nations of the earth would be blessed through the Jewish nation. That blessing was now on the scene, and God wanted this plan to unfold.

When Peter visited Joppa, he went to the roof to pray and fell into a trance. He saw a sheet lowered with various animals the Jews were forbidden to eat. A voice from heaven said to arise, kill, and eat these animals. Peter, being the loyal Jew that he was, refused. The vision happened three times, and God said to him, "What God has cleansed, no longer consider unholy." The barrier between Jew and Gentile was over. God indeed would now pour out His Spirit onto *all* flesh.

This transition would not to be easy. All their lives Jews had been programmed to reject the Gentile, and now they were to accept the Gentile. Think about how hard it is to achieve racial reconciliation in this country. Old prejudices die hard. Yet amid the most intractable differences, God sent His son, Jesus, to be the ultimate unifier of the human race. Peter eventually accepted the invitation from Cornelius to visit his house, and while Peter preached the gospel, the Holy Spirit fell on all the Gentiles present. The kingdom of God was now open to everyone.

Pentecost is also a vivid word picture of what I am saying. People from all over the world were in Jerusalem for the feast (Acts 2:1–8). When the Holy Spirit was poured out, everyone heard the disciples praising God in their own language. The Holy Spirit was the one unifying force that would change history forever. God's passion is that every tribe and every tongue would be included in the family of God.

Consider Peter's words in his first epistle, which highlights the revelation that God gave to him: "For you are a chosen race, a royal priesthood, a holy nation, a people for God's own possession." These words were once exclusively for the Jew, and they now applied to anyone who put his or her trust in Jesus Christ. We now possess the same racial identity because we are the chosen race. Anyone who has been born again has been born to this new race. Let this racial identity supersede your natural biological race. We have the same nationality because we are a part of His holy nation. We are royalty.

We are priests. We are holy. And we belong to Him. We are His possession, and our loyalty must be to Him and Him alone.

One historical incident shows the power of this new heritage that we possess. During World War I at Christmastime in 1914, German and English soldiers climbed out of their trenches to exchange Christmas greetings. At first, the English soldiers noticed little Christmas trees with lights on the top of German trenches. Then the English heard them singing "Silent Night" in German and began to sing along. Finally, a German captain climbed out of the trench with his hands raised. An English captain soon crossed no-man's land to greet the German captain. Soon all the men were out of their trenches exchanging cigarettes, coffee, and other items as goodwill gestures to one another. Their Christian identity overcame their national identity. Sadly, their superior officers ordered the men back to their trenches, and the next day the war resumed. So concerned were the generals from both armies that this spirit of goodwill might spread that they dispersed all the men who witnessed this event to other units in their respective armies. By Christmastime of 1915, most of the men who partook in this historic event were dead. For one brief moment, however, the world had witnessed what the Prince of Peace came to give all men.

Where does your loyalty lie? Is your loyalty to Christ greater than your loyalty to your family, your nation, your race, or your political party? We must elevate our identity to think and to act as that one new man. The unity, which Jesus for in John 17, was intended to sweep all believers into His heavenly embrace and cement our identity in Him.

Imagine if the church could emulate Daniel and fearlessly adhere to our true Christian identity. Think of the great social sins committed in this nation that could be overturned if every Christian exalted loyalty to Christ as their primary virtue. Unfortunately, the enemy still plays the separation game of dividing one Christian camp from the other. Instead, we cling to the lesser loyalties of party, race, and economics to guide our decisions.

We are the light of the world. We are the salt of the earth. When we embrace the heavenly vision of one new man whose true identity is as a son or a daughter of the living God, then we, like Daniel, will have a witness that is ten times better.

CHAPTER 12

YOUR EASTER STORY

THE TURNING POINT OF HISTORY is the death, burial, and resurrection of Jesus Christ. He is the Savior of the world, and He came to set us free from the penalty and the power of sin. Every year at Easter, we focus on this historical event, which defines who we are as Christians. Many churches have dramatic presentations of the three days that changed history. Mel Gibson's movie *The Passion of the Christ*, a worldwide phenomenon, graphically shows the depth of His suffering for mankind. Most Christians would agree that Easter is more important than Christmas because His death, burial, and resurrection have a greater theological importance than the story of His birth. This is not to minimize His virgin birth, but the reason He came to earth was to be the lamb of God who takes away the sin of the world. The Father's ultimate validation for His son was raising Him from the dead.

No other religion has a story like Christianity does. No other religion has a person as magnificent as Jesus. His miracles and His teaching far surpass those of any other religious leader who ever lived. So unique were His miracles that Jesus said if we couldn't believe Him because of the words, we could believe Him based solely on the miraculous works He performed (John 14:11). His final display of divine power was His resurrection from the dead. So amazing was this event that even His disciples had a hard time believing it. Yet it is true. It is the foundation stone of our faith. Paul even said that if there was no resurrection, then our faith is in vain and we are still in our sins.

Think of the lengths that the Jewish leaders went to discredit this event. They paid off the guards who were watching the tomb and told the story that His disciples carried the body away. They knew that the testimony of Jesus rising from the dead would cripple all their plans to silence His memory. In Peter's first two sermons, however, he emphatically proclaims the resurrection and the fact that they were all eyewitnesses to this event:

- **Acts 2:32:** "This Jesus God raised up again, to which we are all witnesses."
- **Acts 3:14–15:** "But you disowned the Holy and Righteous One and asked for a murderer to be granted to you but put to death the Prince of Life, the one God raised from the dead, a fact to which we are all witnesses."

This eyewitness account would be valid today in any court of law. Peter again reiterates his claim of being an eyewitness to this historic event. In 1 Peter 1:16, he declares, "For we did not follow cleverly devised tales when we made known to you the power and coming of our Lord Jesus Christ, but we were eyewitnesses of His majesty."

The assault from the skeptics over the years has never been able to diminish the historical fact that the unique Son of God actually rose from the dead and was witnessed by many people. The church finally coded these historical events in what is now called the Apostles' Creed, which says, "He suffered under Pontius Pilate, was crucified, died, and was buried. He descended into hell; the third day

He arose again from the dead." God sent His son, Jesus, to be the propitiation for our sins and to conquer death.

At gravesides, we hear these words: "O death, where is your victory? O death where is your sting?" Once again we are reminded of the resurrection and Christ's victory over the grave. This truth has echoed down through the centuries and given hope to all mankind. The early Christians' church suffered wave upon wave of persecution because they refused to deny the historical fact of Jesus's death, burial, and resurrection.

The church is right to celebrate this pivotal event. In a world drowning in unbelief, it is fitting for us to proclaim that He is alive. Every person who has ever lived has had to come to grips with the fact that everyone will die. Many delude themselves by thinking that death is the end of everything. Some pin their hopes on reincarnation. Others just choose to ignore it, but the reaper comes for everyone. The Bible clearly states that it is appointed for a man to die once, and after this comes the judgment. The church offers the only hope for people to be free from their sins and to be free from the tyranny of death. God stepped into history and solved once and for all the deepest needs of mankind.

After the church began proclaiming the death, burial, and resurrection of Jesus Christ, the apostle Paul took that historical event and revealed to us that His story is now our story.

Listen to how he describes our total identification with Christ in His death, burial, and resurrection in his various letters:

* **Romans 6:4–6:** "Therefore we have been buried with Him through baptism into death, so that as Christ was raised from the dead through the glory of the Father, so we too might walk in newness of life. For if we become united with Him in the likeness of His death, certainly we shall also be in the

likeness of His resurrection. Knowing this, that our old self was crucified with Him, in order that our body of sin might be done away, so that we would no longer be slaves to sin."

* **Galatians 2:20:** "I have been crucified with Christ; and it is no longer I who live, but Christ lives in me; and the life I now live in the flesh I live by faith in the Son of God, who loved me and gave Himself up for me."

* **Colossians 2:10–12:** "And in Him you have been made complete, and He is the head over all rule and authority; and in Him you were also circumcised with a circumcision made without hands, in the removal of the body of the flesh by the circumcision of Christ; having been buried with Him in baptism, in which you were also raised up with Him through faith in the working of God, who raised Him from the dead."

Look at this level of identification. I have been crucified with Christ. I have been buried with Christ, and finally, I have been raised up with Christ. What was once history is now my testimony. His Easter story is now my Easter story.

I believe Paul received these revelations during one of his prolonged absences from the church. In Galatians 1:15–2:1–2, he says the following:

But when God, who had set me apart even from my mother's womb and called me through His grace, was pleased to reveal His Son in me so that I might preach Him among the Gentiles, I did not immediately consult with flesh and blood, nor did I go up to Jerusalem to those who were apostles before me; but I went away to Arabia, and returned once more to Damascus. Then three years later I went up to Jerusalem to become acquainted with Cephas, and stayed with him fifteen days. But I did not see any other of the apostles except James, the Lord's brother. (Now in what I am writing to you, I assure you before God that I am not lying.) Then I went into the regions of Syria and Cilicia. I was still unknown by sight in the churches of Judea which were in Christ; but only, they kept hearing, "He who once persecuted us is now preaching the faith which he once tried to destroy." And they were glorifying God because of me. Then after an interval of fourteen years I went up again to Jerusalem with Barnabas, taking Titus along also. It was because of a revelation that I went up; and I submitted to them the gospel which I preach among the Gentiles, but I did so in private to those who were of reputation, for fear that I might be running, or had run, in vain.

I believe Paul received such a heavenly download of revelation of our identity that he saw the bigger picture of what Christ had accomplished. Not only did Paul see the fullness of the gospel of God's grace, but he also saw our complete identification in the death, burial, and resurrection of Jesus Christ. Even Peter said that some of the things God had showed Paul were hard for him to understand (2 Pet. 3:16). Peter was a physical witness of the death, burial, and resurrection of Jesus Christ, and Paul, by the Spirit, was able to witness our death, our burial, and our resurrection in Christ. The typical greeting on Easter morning is "He is risen," and we all reply, "He is risen indeed." We can now add this to our chorus: "We have risen." And we can all joyously reply, "We have risen indeed!"

CHAPTER 13

BREAKING THE
ORPHAN SPIRIT

JESUS SAID, "I WILL NOT leave you as orphans but I will come to you" (John 14:18). The reason God sent His son into the world was to adopt a planet of orphans. To everyone who receives Jesus as their Lord and Savior, He gave them the right to become sons of God. The spirit of adoption has now replaced the spirit of slavery, and we are now part of His amazing family with God Himself as our father.

When Adam and Eve fell, they not only lost Paradise—they also lost their father and their family. Mankind's lost position before God became the fertile ground for the orphan spirit to grow. Sin has driven us away from His loving embrace. Adam once walked with God in confidence and security, but now he has descended into fear and insecurity. The good news of the gospel is that God has removed the impediment of sin and put out the welcome mat for all the orphans to return home.

In John, chapter 14, Jesus begins to highlight how the Trinity—the Father, the Son, and the Holy Spirit—will all be employed to crush the orphan spirit. Every Christian must be rightly related to all three persons in the Trinity to walk in his or her true redeemed value. We need the Father to validate us that we are His beloved children. We then need the Son to help us overcome our weakness as our faithful high priest, and we need the Holy Spirit to bear witness to our spirit that we are the children of God. Each relationship enhances our standing as sons and daughters and not as orphans. I want to take a deeper look at the interaction of the Trinity in this process.

THE FATHER'S ROLE IN CRUSHING THE ORPHAN SPIRIT

The sweetest words the Father can hear are spoken when His lost children return and call Him "Abba." The Bible declares that God is love, and it was this love that motivated the Father to send His son to reclaim lost humanity. The deep cry of the Father's heart was to bring many sons to glory (Heb. 2:10). When Jesus talked about prayer, He deepened our understanding of our relationship with God by inviting us to call Him "Our Father."

Everyone needs a father. From fathers we receive identity and validation. Fathers enhance their daughters' beauty and femininity, and they enhance their sons' strength and masculinity. Look at the validation the Father gave to Jesus at His baptism. "This is My beloved Son in whom I am well pleased." Without the Father's validation, we are left questioning our value and our worth.

Jesus's insight into our value to the Father is highlighted in His words: "Just as the Father has loved me, so have I loved you." We all have the same access to the Father's heart as Jesus has. Many of us have father wounds from our natural fathers. These wounds often become roadblocks to accessing the love and validation we need from God our Father. In Hebrews (12:9–10), the writer states that we have earthly fathers who discipline us as best as they can, but now our real Father dispenses perfect discipline to be like Him in His holiness. The only pathway to freedom from the abuse and neglect of our earthly fathers is to forgive them and embrace the Father we always longed for.

The primary meaning of "forgive" is "to send away." When God forgave our sins, He sent them away as far as the east is from the west, never to be remembered again. It was like the scapegoat in the Old Testament. On the Day of Atonement, the scapegoat was sent out of the camp of the Israelites, illustrating that their sins had been sent away (Lev. 16:8–10). By forgiving your natural father, you are sending away the pain and the power of that relationship to continue to hurt you. Say good-bye to disappointment and heartache and say hello to the reality that you are now the son or daughter in whom He is well pleased. You can now enter into that joyous place where you are "daily His delight, rejoicing always before Him" (Prov. 8:30).

JESUS'S ROLE IN OUR ADOPTION

Jesus is our loyal brother and our faithful high priest. Everyone needs someone who can relate to his or her fears and failures. Jesus became man so that He could uniquely satisfy the demands of God and the needs of man. Once we have been justified by faith, we need an ally in our struggle with the flesh—not just an ally but a sympathetic ally, one who has also been tempted in everything we are going through yet who is without sin. Our sins and failures become the arsenal for the enemy to attack us with condemnation. Satan is relentless in accusing us of our sins and failures and reminding us that we are still sinners. This is where Jesus comes to the rescue. He shows us the way of escape from temptation. He encourages us by reminding us that He can rescue the godly from temptation.

Every time we sin, we feel compelled to return to the orphanage and surrender our adoption papers. We find ourselves singing the same tune as the prodigal son sang when he returned and said, "I am not worthy to be your son; make me as one of your hired servants." This is the anthem of all spiritual orphans. Proverbs 24:16 declares that the righteous man falls seven times but gets back up. Our sins do not disqualify us from sonship but provide the opportunity for God's grace to abound to us. Again, this is not an excuse to sin but our hope in our struggle against sin.

I marvel at the way Jesus related to people. He was disparagingly called the "friend of sinners." Yet that title is our hope and our home. He is our true friend who can relate to our struggles and at the same time lead us to victory. The ultimate challenge for the children of God is to maintain their identity as righteous sons and daughters as they struggle with unrighteousness. We have been given the righteousness of Christ, and the blood of Jesus Christ still cleanses us from all unrighteousness. When we find ourselves declaring that we are just helpless sinners, we have unconsciously separated ourselves from His gracious help. Don't let these declarations become your identity.

A hurricane of lies from the enemy combined with our own unrighteous thoughts wage war with our secure standing as children of God. We must learn to take these thoughts captive, or they will inflame that orphan spirit. Talk to Jesus about the sin that so easily entangles you. Don't just ask for forgiveness and promise not to do it again but employ the one who is qualified to show you how to walk in victory in that specific area. Remember, He became you so you could become Him. He is not ashamed to call you brethren (Heb. 2:11). We may be ashamed when we fall, but He never is. He is like that parent who patiently helps his child to walk because he knows the potential in that child to walk.

THE HOLY SPIRIT AND THE SPIRIT OF ADOPTION

The Holy Spirit is the most amazing member of the Trinity in our struggle to overcome the orphan spirit. As I said before, when we are born again, the Holy Spirit bears witness with our spirit that we are children of God (Rom. 8:13). He is our surety or our down payment for connecting us to our heavenly Father and His son, Jesus Christ. We have the forgiveness of sins and the gift of eternal life. He empowers us to lead effective Christian lives by saturating us with Himself when we are baptized in the Holy Spirit.

He is the one Jesus referred to when He said, "I will not leave you as orphans." He is the spirit of adoption rescuing us from the orphanage of sin. He is ever reminding us of our true standing before God—that we are now accepted and not rejected. The main strategy of Satan is separation. When he was the garden, his main goal was separating Adam and Eve from God. He succeeded, and every generation since has been born with a sense of alienation from God. Man is still hiding from the one who wants to adopt him. We are so used to living as orphans that it takes an amazing amount of reassurance to believe that we are truly reconciled to God Himself. Many live their lives with a sense that their adoption is conditional and that one slipup will send them back to the orphanage. We swing back and forth between "He loves me" one day only to declare, "He loves me not" the next day.

The modern practice of adoption is far different from the Roman practice of adoption. Paul wrote to many churches governed by Roman law, and he used this analogy to anchor the church's understanding of the power of adoption. In Roman times, if a prominent family had no sons or had sons who were considered inferior in character, the family could disown that son and adopt a stranger in his place. If you ever have seen the movie *Ben-Hur*, you may remember that this is what happened to Judah Ben-Hur. He was a slave who was adopted by a counsel of Rome. He was no longer a slave but took on the name of this prominent Roman general, and all of this man's estate belonged to him.

In the Roman adoption process, all your former debts were canceled. In reality, you started a new life. According to Roman law, only natural sons could be disowned or forsaken. A legally adopted son could never be disowned.

The parallels between Roman adoption and what God did for us are staggering. The Father disowned His own son, Jesus, to legally adopt you and me. When Jesus cried out, "My God, My God why have you forsaken me?" He was momentarily disowned by the Father because of our sin. Once He rose from the dead, He assumed the position of our brother and joint heir. The good news of the gospel is that we can never be disowned. That is the power of adoption.

Another great weapon to dismantle the orphan spirit is love. Only by knowing that you are unconditionally loved can you pry your heart and mind from the habit of living like an orphan. Romans 5:5 declares that "for we know how dearly God loves us, and we feel this warm love everywhere within us because God has given us the Holy Spirit to fill our hearts with His love" (Living Bible). In other translations it says that the love of God has been "poured out" or "shed abroad" in hearts by the Holy Spirit. The Greek word "ekcheo" gives the sense of something gushing out. Think of an oil well that has been tapped. A gusher shoots high into the air, and the company is rich beyond its wildest dreams. In the same way, God's loves will explode the orphan spirit within you. Picture yourself under Niagara Falls, and it will give you an idea of that kind of love. This is the kind of love that Paul said we should be "rooted and grounded" in. He goes on to pray that all of us may be able to comprehend what is the breadth, and length, and height, and depth of His love. So amazing is His love and acceptance that it even surpasses knowledge. We need a fresh revelation of this kind of love. Ask the Lord to help you comprehend His love. When you truly know that you are loved, you will know for sure that you are no longer an orphan. You have the Father, the Son, and the Holy Spirit who are ready and willing to bring you home.

One of the easiest ways to know that you have an orphan spirit is to recognize your inability to "rejoice with those who rejoice" (Rom. 12:15). The older brother in the parable about the prodigal son demonstrated this clearly. He could not enter into the joy of his brother's return. He reasoned that a celebration for his brother must mean the father did not want to celebrate him.

The orphan spirit will always tell you that there is a limited supply of God's love and resources. If someone else is being blessed, then it must mean that there is less for you. Resentment, jealousy, and bitterness are all telltale signs that the orphan spirit still clings to your identity. Your ability to rejoice with those who rejoice is evidence of your confidence in a loving Father who has enough blessings for all His children. Remember, you are always a candidate for God's blessings. He determines the size and measure of the blessing, but His heart is to bless every one of His own.

CHAPTER 14

FROM APPROVAL VERSUS FOR APPROVAL

IF YOU LIVE YOUR LIFE in the light of His approval, you can change your world. Jesus began His ministry with a resounding shout of approval from His heavenly Father. But this was not the only time we see the Father affirming and validating Jesus as His beloved. On the Mount of Transfiguration, when Moses and Elijah appeared with Jesus, we hear the Father again say, "This is My beloved Son, with whom I am well pleased; listen to Him" (Matt. 17:1–8). No temptation from Satan or the accolades from the crowd to make Him king could move Jesus from His father's approval. Jesus had no ear for the father of lies or the transitory approval of men. Being rooted in His Father's love and approval became the bedrock of His ministry. Because of this, He was able to withstand the crashing waves of opposition challenging His calling to be the savior of the world. If Jesus needed to hear these words of approval more than once, how much more often do we need to hear them?

Mankind is on a desperate search for approval. Since the fall of Adam and Eve, we have been dominated by fear and insecurity. Unsure of God's approval, we seek others' approval. Being neglected or rejected in our youth will further push us to try to earn the approval of others. Some of us are trapped in being people pleasers. We find it impossible to say no to others because we cannot afford their disapproval. Children long for the approval of their mother and father and will often go to great lengths to achieve it. People often go to their graves with a deep heartache because of the lack of parental approval. This longing for approval is, deep down, the heart's cry for God's approval. For only under His approving gaze do we find the ultimate security we so urgently seek.

How do you live your Christian life? Now that you know God as our Savior, do you still feel compelled to perform for His approval? Why do you still labor for what is already yours? This is the tyranny of legalism. Most of us are mired in performance-based living. The grace that calls us unconditionally is soon replaced by the law. We do not consciously subscribe to the law, but the church puts such emphasis on behavior that it naturally moves us in that direction. We still long for His approval, and thus perform for His approval. True freedom is when we live *from* approval, not *for* approval. Jesus modeled this lifestyle for us and encourages us to follow Him because His father is now our Father.

The Protestant Reformation began when Martin Luther discovered the marvelous truth that "the just shall live by faith" (Rom. 1:17). He clearly saw that we are justified in the sight of God by putting our faith in Jesus Christ and His atoning work. His righteousness has now become our righteousness. Righteousness by faith and not by works was the battle cry of the Reformation. Although many other truths came to light at this time, this was the central point of contention with the established church.

Most of us look at the Reformation as a battle over doctrine and theology, but the Reformation began when Luther discovered God's smile. Consider his words in describing his insight into Romans 1:17:

I greatly longed to understand Paul's epistle to the Romans and nothing stood in the way but that one expression, "the justice of God," because I took it to mean that justice whereby God is just and deals justly in punishing the unjust. My situation was that, although an impeccable monk, I stood before God as a sinner troubled in conscience, and I had no confidence that my merit would assuage him. Therefore I did not love a just and angry God, but rather hated and murmured against him. Yet I clung to the dear Paul and had a great yearning to know what he meant.

Night and day I pondered until I saw the connection between the justice of God and the statement that "the just shall live by faith." Then I grasped that the justice of God is that righteousness by which through grace and sheer mercy God justifies us through faith. Thereupon I felt myself to be reborn and to have gone through open doors into paradise. The whole of scripture took on a new meaning, and whereas before the "justice of God" had filled me with hate, now it became to me inexpressibly sweet in greater love. This passage of Paul became to me a gate to heaven...

If you have true faith that Christ is your Savior, then at once you have a gracious God, for faith leads you in and opens up God's heart and will, that you should see pure grace and overflowing love. This is to behold God in faith that you should look upon his fatherly, friendly heart in which there is no anger nor ungraciousness. He who sees God as angry does not see rightly but looks only on a curtain, as if a dark cloud had been drawn across his face. (Bainton 1950, 51)

Luther became enraptured with God's friendly face. Because of what Christ had done, God's disapproval soon melted into unconditional approval. Stop for a moment and ponder his "fatherly, friendly heart." Can you see Him smiling at you? This is why Luther could withstand the furnace blast of opposition from the church. It was more than a battle over theology. It was the loving gaze of God that held him for the rest of his life.

I find it interesting that the focus on the Reformation still centers on the doctrinal aspects of this battle. I am not minimizing these truths, but we never hear Luther's revelation in its fullness. How did we become champions of justification by faith and lose sight of His gracious face? Many Christians are stuck in condemnation and sin consciousness, and they work hard for their heavenly Father's approval. Let a new reformation of our identity in Christ and His gracious acceptance of us take root and grow.

Another one of my champions of faith is George Müller. He was a nineteenth-century English pastor who made his reputation by caring for more than ten thousand orphans in the city of Bristol. His reputation as a man of faith is without equal. He never once asked for financial support but simply prayed and believed God would supply all the funds needed to sustain the ministry.

Following is the popular story of his childlike trust in God's provision: One morning when the orphanage had no bread or milk for breakfast, he had the three hundred orphans bow their heads and say a blessing over their breakfast. While they were praying, there was a knock at the door. First, a local baker said that the Lord woke him in the middle of the night and told him to bake sufficient bread for the orphans that day. Next, a man with a milk wagon said that he had just broken a wheel in front of the orphanage and wanted to know if he could give them all his milk because the milk would spoil while he waited to have the wheel fixed. One can only imagine the challenge to eventually care for over ten thousand orphans.

How did George Müller see God? These are his own words describing the secret to his ministry and his walk with God:

> According to my judgment the most important point to be attended to is this: above all things see to it that your souls are happy in the Lord. Other things may press upon you, the Lord's work may even have urgent claims upon your attention, but I deliberately repeat, it is of supreme and paramount importance that you should seek above all things to have your souls truly happy in God Himself! Day by day seek to make this the most important business of your life. This has been my firm and settled condition for the last five and thirty years. For the first four years after my conversion I knew not its vast importance, but now after much experience I specially commend this point to the notice of my younger brethren and sisters in Christ: *the secret of all true effectual service is joy in God*, having experimental acquaintance and fellowship with God Himself. (Muller 1878)

We cannot get happy in the Lord when we are covered in condemnation. Unless we see His smiling face and His approving gaze, we leave our time with Him to join the rest of the older brothers who are slavishly trying to work for His approval. Oh, to come home to the approval of a loving Father! How the world needs to see Him through our joy. What an invitation that would be to all the orphans who are looking for a true father and a real home to warm their weary hearts. In His presence is the fullness of joy, not the fullness of rejection or the fullness of condemnation. Come on, church—get happy in the Lord.

Listen to the words of the Aaronic blessing found in Numbers 6:24–26 that God commanded Moses to say over the nation of Israel:

The Lord bless you, and keep you;
The Lord make His face shine (smile) on you,
And be gracious to you;
The Lord lift up His countenance on you,
And give you peace.

I love how the Living Bible translates verse 25: "May the Lord's face radiate with joy because of you."

Have you ever noticed how we instinctively smile at babies? I believe that smile is rooted in God's smile for you. As much as a baby needs to know the approval of others, we need that same approval from God. We are drawn to smiles, and we are drawn to laughter and joy. Walk into a room of people, and if there are some people laughing, we are instantly drawn to where the laughter is occurring. Laughter, joy, and smiles are all safe places for the human heart to hang out. Both Luther and Müller found this safe place with God. It was from this place that they changed their world. Let's start living our lives from approval, not for approval.

CHAPTER 15

SEEING IS RECEIVING

How we see God is how we receive from God. If we see Him as a gracious and generous Father, then our faith will rise to claim His abundant promises. On the other hand if we see Him as a reluctant lord, then we will rarely use our faith to access our inheritance. Jesus highlighted this dynamic in the story of the talents in Matthew 25:14–30:

> For it is just like a man about to go on a journey, who called his own slaves and entrusted his possessions to them.
>
> To one he gave five talents, to another, two, and to another, one, each according to his ability; and he went on his journey.
>
> Immediately the one who had received the five talents went and traded with them, and gained five more talents.
>
> In the same manner the one who received the two talents gained two more.
>
> But he who received the one talent went away, and dug a hole in the ground and hid his master's money.
>
> Now after a long time the master of those slaves came and settled accounts with them.
>
> To the one who had received the five talents came up and brought five more talents, saying, "Master, you entrusted five talents to me. See I have gained five more talents."

His master said to him, "Well done, good and faithful slave. You were faithful with a few things; enter into the joy of your master." Also the one who received the two talents came up and said, "Master, you have entrusted two talents to me. See, I have gained two more talents."

His master said to him, "Well done, good and faithful slave. You were faithful with a few things, I will put you in charge of many things; enter into the joy of your master." And the one who received the one talent came up and said, "Master, I knew you to be a hard man, reaping where you did not sow and gathering where you scattered no seed. And I was afraid, and went away and hid your talent in the ground. See, you have what is yours."

But his master answered and said to him, "You wicked and lazy slave, you knew that I reap where I did not sow and gather where I scattered no seed.

"Then you ought to have put my money in the bank, and on my arrival I would have received my money back with interest.

"Therefore take away the talent from him and give it to the one who has the ten talents." For to everyone who has, more shall be given, and the one who does not have, even what he does have shall be taken away.

"Throw out the worthless slave into outer darkness; in the place there will be weeping and gnashing of teeth."

This parable is as sobering as it is insightful. God has provided a rich inheritance for all His children. He has also given us gifts and graces designed to bless others and expand His kingdom. In addition, He has a strong expectation that we learn how to access our inheritance and use our talents for His glory.

For me, the key word in this parable is "immediately" in verse 16. This word tells me that the servant with the five talents had a correct view of His master. The servant saw Him as generous and empowering. This viewpoint enabled him to take risks and trade with the money given to him. A talent in biblical times was worth about a day's wage. Apparently, the servant with the two talents had that same viewpoint about his master because he operated in "the same manner" as the man with five talents (verse 17). Seeing God correctly will inspire our faith and motivate us to take risks in our adventures with God. Whether we are praying for the sick or believing for some new ministry, we must operate with confidence that God will bless our endeavors. "This I know that God is for me" (Ps. 56:9) must be the banner we march under.

On the other hand, we see the servant with one talent and his warped view of His master. "I knew you to be a hard man" (verse 24) was the banner he marched under. This distorted viewpoint caused him to operate out of fear. Fear will always give you a shovel to bury your talents. Fear will always paralyze you, preventing you from acting boldly and taking risks for the kingdom.

Each of us has an amazing destiny with God. His plans for your life are greater than you can imagine. But so many of us have been offended by God because of past disappointments or unanswered prayers. This provides the enemy with an opportunity to take his vile paintbrush and paint a twisted portrait of our heavenly Father. Instead of being "ten talent" Christians, we put our destiny on hold. If we do have a clouded view of God, it's time to cry out like blind Bartimaeus, who said to Jesus, "Lord, I want to see" (Luke 18:41). We must see Him clearly. We must see Him as good. Like David, we must be able to say, "I believed I would see the goodness of God in the land of the living" (Ps. 27:13).

Once, the Lord had to rescue me from my own limited view of His goodness. While working in Spain as a missionary, I met my wife, Beth. She was working in the school the mission was running.

Needless to say, I was thrilled with the Lord's choice for me. It was truly a supernatural courtship. We never dated, but the Lord confirmed to each of our hearts that we were to be married. It was as unusual as it was adventurous. After we compared everything the Lord was speaking to us about, we declared our engagement. I then started thinking about getting Beth an engagement ring. At first I rejected this thought as materialistic and worldly. We were missionaries and needed no such adornment. Or so I thought. But I was confused.

I had left everything in the States to go to the mission field. Even when I got to Spain, the Lord challenged me to give everything away and trust Him completely. I thought I had made great strides in this area. I thought that asking God for a diamond ring for Beth would be met with His disapproval. I often saw my walk with God like the child's board game Chutes and Ladders. In this game you roll the dice and move along the board. Sometimes you land on a spot and find a ladder that takes you higher. Sometimes you land on a spot with a chute that drops you lower on the board. I thought asking God for a diamond ring would put me in a chute to lower spirituality or carnality. But I also had no peace with not getting Beth a ring.

One night I went out alone to pray about this situation. I thought the Lord would be disappointed that I would even bring it up. I finally said, "Lord, what do You think about me getting Beth a diamond engagement ring?" What He said changed forever the way I looked at God: "Tim, I would withhold nothing from my bride. Get the ring!" Within six weeks, the Lord miraculously provided the resources and the ring. What a matchmaker! What a God!

As a Christian, you are the bride of Christ. He has withheld nothing from you. He has provided and will provide for every need. He is more than generous. He is more than good. He is much better than we think.

CHAPTER 16

HEIRS LIVING LIKE SLAVES

"Now I say as long as the heir is a child, he does not differ at all from a slave although he is the owner of everything" (Gal. 4:1, NASB).

The context of the opening verse is that before grace came, we were held under the tutorship of the law. For many Christians, unfortunately, they have not learned to make the transition from slave to heir. We live our lives dominated by our behavior rather by than our identity. Let us continue with Paul's letter:

> But when the fullness of time came, God sent forth His Son, born of a woman, born under the Law, so that He might redeem those who are under the Law, that we might receive the adoption as sons. Because you are sons, God has sent forth the Spirit of His Son into our hearts, crying, "Abba! Father!" Therefore you are no longer a slave, but a son, and if a son, then an heir through God. (Gal. 4:4–7, NASB)

When your primary focus is on your behavior, you become ensnared in the law. This is why many Christians live under condemnation. We can only achieve righteous behavior through our new righteous identity. What truth demands, grace supplies. I look to Him and not myself. Legalism is just as prevalent today as it was when Jesus walked the earth. The Pharisaical spirit is alive and well in the body of Christ. We are all tempted to take the shortcut to righteousness by conformity to outward standards.

Consider Paul's admonition to the Colossians:

> If you have died with Christ to the elementary principle of the world, why, as if you were living in the world, do you submit yourself to decrees, such as, "Do not handle, do not taste, do not touch!" (which all refer to things destined to perish with use)—in accordance with the commandments and teachings of men? These are matters which have, to be sure, the appearance of wisdom in self-made religion and the self-abasement and severe treatment of the body, but are of no value against fleshly indulgence. (Col. 2:20–23)

Stop living as a slave. Stop living as a child. "We are to *grow up* into *all* aspects into Him" (Eph. 4:15, emphasis mine). All means all. Every aspect of Jesus's life is now available to us. His righteous character is now ours. His demonstration of kingdom power and provision is now ours. We must not settle for anything less.

Let's take a look at the characteristics of children that hinder us from living as heirs. First, children are impatient. They want what they want *now*. Have you ever seen a child throw a tantrum while negotiating for candy on display in the checkout line? Many of us have attempted to live like heirs only to become frustrated and give up. We make up a theology that discounts living like an heir in order to justify our impatience, and then we attack those who do lay claim to the inheritance. It is "by faith *and patience*" that we inherit the promises.

The second characteristic that hinders us is a childlike lack of knowledge. The church has not been successful in bringing people to maturity because we lack an understanding of our true identity. We still brand saints as sinners, which leads us all back to legalism, not freedom. We still equate inheritance with greed, which keeps us locked in an impoverished mind-set. We still proclaim that the miraculous is not for today, which keeps us sick. Only the truth will set us free. The traditions of man have superseded the word of God and left us as children. All the promises of God are designed for us to become partakers of His divine nature. Immerse yourself in the word of God and lay claim to all that is yours.

The third characteristic that hinders us is a childlike subordination to the senses. They use what they see, what they hear, what they feel, what they taste, and what they smell to negotiate life. True maturity for a Christian is a life dominated by faith, not by sight. "The just will live by faith" is our mandate. Our faith must go beyond salvation and press on to the high ground of our inheritance. Faith is the passport to kingdom living. Our faith pleases Him because we go beyond our senses. Eve "saw" that the tree was good. She put her trust in creation, not the Creator. Faith reunites us with the Creator and unlocks our inheritance.

One of the saddest stories in scripture is when the nation of Israel failed to take the Promised Land. Moses sent out twelve spies to survey the land. On their return, ten of the spies discouraged the people from going forward. The prize was obvious to them but their identity was not. "We are like grasshoppers" was their estimation of their identity. Joshua and Caleb had a true sense of their godly heritage and declared, "We are more than able to take the land." Having a "more than able" mind-set is required for all who want to live like heirs. Sure, there are obstacles, but we feed our faith by overcoming every one of them. Israel's diminished identity kept the Israelites from their prize for another forty years. They were heirs living like slaves in the wilderness. Let us not imitate them but put aside all childish things and lay claim to our full inheritance.

CHAPTER 17

STAY IN YOUR ASSIGNED SEAT

THE WORD OF GOD STATES that we are "seated with Christ in heavenly places" (Eph. 2:6). This was accomplished by His death on the cross and by your faith in His atoning sacrifice. Your faith now became your righteousness standing before God (Gal. 2:16). This is the most amazing gift that God could ever give: His own righteousness to those who simply believe. This revelation of righteousness given to Martin Luther inspired the Protestant Reformation. I marvel at this great gift to mankind. God justifies the ungodly (Rom. 4:5). He made ungodly people godly by His work of redemption. This gift is offered to any and all who believe. Now that we have the righteousness of Christ imputed to us, we are now seated together with Him. This seat is our new home, but sadly, many Christians do not know how to remain there. We need a deeper understanding of righteousness and how to live *from* righteousness, not *for* righteousness.

I use the following illustration in my church to help people understand their new standing in Christ. I place two chairs side by side on the platform. One chair is labeled "sinner" and the other chair is labeled "righteous." I explain that before we come to Christ, we are seated in the sinner chair. Once we put our faith in Christ as our Savior, we are assigned to the righteous chair. We are seated together with Him. Our identity is now rooted in the fact that we have been washed and that we have been sanctified by Christ (1 Cor. 6:11). His righteousness is now my righteousness. His seat is now my seat.

Imagine you are boarding a plane, and your boarding pass says that you are seated in the coach section. As you board the plane, you see the people seated in the first-class section. They have nice, wide chairs and plenty of legroom. Many already have their beverage and snacks while you are still lugging your carry-on bags to your seat. Suppose you stop in first class and ask a woman seated if you may have her seat. What would be her reply? She would tell you that this is her assigned seat and that she paid for it and is not going to move. On any flight, we are required to sit in our assigned seat.

I use this illustration to show saints not to move out of their assigned seats of righteousness even when they sin. Satan comes along after we have sinned, and he tells us to get up and return to the sinner seat. Most Christians do this without realizing what has happened. They do it because they do not fully understand their true righteous standing before God. Justification is the process in which God declares you holy and righteous. You are no longer sinners but now saints of God. "Just as if they never sinned" is an apt definition of justification. Christ alone has done the work of justification.

Sanctification is the process in which our lives conform to the righteous character of God Himself. Our lives now mimic Him. This is not accomplished through human effort but through the sanctifying work of God's Spirit alive in every believer. All we need is to yield our wills to the prompting of the Holy Spirit and to walk in obedience in that area. He does the work. Consider these verses, which highlight this point:

* **Ephesians 2:10:** "For we are God's masterpiece. He has created us anew in Christ Jesus, so we can do the things he planned for us long ago" (NLT).

- **Philippians 2:13:** "For God is working in you, giving you the desire and the power to do what pleases him" (NLT).
- **Hebrews 13:21:** "May he equip you with everything you need for doing his will. May he produce in you, through the power of Jesus Christ, every good thing that is pleasing to him. All the glory to him forever and ever! Amen" (NLT).

He does the work in our justification and our sanctification. All we need to do is abide in Him and His word, and righteous fruit will grow. By faith and obedience, we will see our lives coming into conformity to His. And when we do sin, we have an advocate with the Father to forgive us and let us continue to walk in the paths of righteousness for His name's sake. Staying rooted in the fact that you are righteous even when you sin will empower you to live righteously. Switching seats is a switch of identity. Trying to live righteously with the identity of a sinner is practically impossible when you put the emphasis on your behavior to achieve the righteous standing that you already have.

Let me give you an example from scripture. In John 13:5–11, we have the scene of Jesus washing the disciples' feet:

Then He poured water into the basin, and began to wash the disciples' feet and to wipe them with the towel with which He was girded. So He came to Simon Peter. He said to Him, "Lord, do you wash my feet?" Jesus answered and said to him, "What I do you do not realize now, but you will understand hereafter." Peter said to Him, "Never shall you wash my feet!" Jesus answered him, "If I do not wash you, you have no part with Me." Simon Peter said to Him, "Lord, then wash not only my feet, but also my hands and my head." Jesus said to him, "He who has bathed needs only to wash his feet, but is completely clean, and you are clean, but not all of you." For He knew the one who was betraying Him; for this reason He said, "Not all of you are clean."

I want to draw your attention to the most important point of this story. Jesus said that they would not understand what He was doing now, but they would understand later. Obviously He wasn't talking about washing feet. They were all familiar with this custom. In biblical days, foot washing was performed in every household, usually by the servants. So what was the deeper revelation that Jesus wanted them to understand? Jesus shows us that when we sin we do not forfeit our righteous standing before Him. "He who has bathed needs only to wash his feet, *but is completely clean, and you are clean*" (John 13:10) (emphasis mine). Like Peter, we assume we need to be bathed all over again when only our feet need to be cleansed.

We have all been baptized into Christ. We were washed, and we were sanctified by Him. Occasionally we may step off the paths of righteousness into unrighteousness, but our sin does not disqualify us from our righteous standing before God. "If we confess our sins, He is faithful and righteous to forgive us our sins and to *cleanse* us from all unrighteousness" (1 John 1:9, emphasis mine). We stay seated in our chairs and extend our feet for Jesus to wash them, safe in the knowledge that we are completely clean.

To remain seated in our identity as a saint, we must never yield to the voice of condemnation. The word of God must drown out the lies of the accuser. "There is therefore now *no condemnation* for those who are in Christ Jesus, for the law of the Spirit and Life in Christ Jesus has set you free from the law of sin and death" (Rom. 8:1, emphasis mine). We must also reject any thought that would displace us from our true place in Christ. Let the confidence that was in the apostle Paul spill over into your heart when he so boldly declared, "For I am confident in this very thing, that He who began a good work in you will perfect it until the day of Christ Jesus" (Phil. 1:6)

CHAPTER 18

FULL COVERAGE

OVER A SERIES OF MONTHS in 1979, Roland Buck, a pastor from Iowa, had amazing visitations from angels. He related these encounters in his book *Angels on Assignment*. Some may find the idea of someone having angelic visitations strange, but in Hebrews 13:2, it says, "Do not neglect to show hospitality to strangers, for by this some of have entertained angels without knowing it." For the most part, Buck's angelic encounters only amplified biblical truths we already know or have neglected to teach. One particular revelation came from the angel Gabriel, who wanted Buck to know God's view of His people. The angel said most people believe that God sees them the way they see themselves with their sins, faults, and failures. However, when God sees you, He sees you through the lens of the blood of His son, Jesus. He sees you as perfect, holy, blameless, and without reproach. Although most of us believe this to be true, we still can't shake the condemnation and guilt that tugs at our hearts.

The angel drew the pastor's attention to Numbers 23:19–23 to enhance his understanding of God's perspective. This was the story of King Balak, who hired the prophet Balaam to curse Israel when the Israelites came to the land. Balaam then began to prophesy blessings on Israel instead of curses:

God is not a man that He should lie, nor the son of man that He should repent; Has He said, and will He not do it? Or has He spoken and will He not make it good.

Behold, I have received a command to bless; When He has blessed, then I cannot revoke it.

He has not observed misfortune in Jacob; Nor has He seen trouble in Israel; The Lord his God is with him, And the shout of a king is among them.

God brings them out of Egypt, He is for them like the horns of a wild ox.

For there is no omen against Jacob, Nor is there any divination against Israel; At the proper time it shall be said to Jacob And to Israel, what God has done!

The angel drew Buck's attention to verse 21 because this was God's perspective on the nation of Israel: "He has not observed misfortune in Jacob." The word "misfortune" can also be translated as iniquity, wickedness, or unrighteousness. God saw no wickedness or iniquity in His people. He also saw no trouble in Israel. Because of this God was positioned to bless His people, not curse them.

To further appreciate this perspective, all we have to do is look at the Passover. Before the Israelites left Egypt, they were required to eat the Passover meal. They were instructed to take the blood of the lamb they had eaten and put the blood on the doorposts of their homes. When the angel of death passed over and saw the blood, the firstborn of that house would be spared. No judgment would visit that home. It didn't matter if the husband and the wife of that home had just had a fight or if the children had misbehaved or if there had been some other domestic dispute. All God saw was the blood, and that satisfied Him.

The apostle Paul draws our attention to this covering that was over Israel. In 1 Corinthians 10:1–6 we read the following: "For I do not want you to be unaware, brethren, that our fathers were all under the cloud and all passed through the sea; and all were baptized into Moses in the cloud and in the sea; and all ate the same spiritual food; and all drank the same spiritual drink, for they were drinking from a spiritual rock which followed them; and the rock was Christ."

While we remain under the covering of God, we can relax. He chose us before the foundation of the world so that we should be holy and blameless before Him (Eph. 1:4). We have no fear because the atonement of Jesus is now our covering. God is holy and can only dwell where sin is covered. Our sins are now covered. We are the temples of God because of what Jesus did on the cross. The measure of our lives is not what we have done but what He has done for us.

This does not mean that God is not interested in our behavior. He longs for us to grow up and produce the fruit of the spirit. Our character should eventually match His character. In our journey into maturity, there is abundant grace and forgiveness.

The only thing that can pull us out from under His covering is outright rebellion or idolatry. King Balak failed to get Balaam to curse the nation of Israel, so Balaam devised a new plan. He enticed the Jewish men to have relations with the women of Moab (Rev. 2:14). Because of this gross unrepentant sin, God judged Israel. So bold was their rebellion that one of the men from Israel took a Moabite woman, marched right past Moses and the leaders of Israel, and went into his tent to have sexual relations with her. Phinehas, the son of Eleazar, the son of Aaron, was so alarmed that he took a javelin, went into the tent, and thrust them both through. All told, twenty-four thousand men of Israel died from the plague because of their sin. Habitual, unrepentant sin will place your position with

God in deep jeopardy. Eternal security is a person, not a doctrine. As long as we remain faithful to Him, we have nothing to fear.

As far as the east is from the west, so far has He removed our transgressions from us (Ps. 103:12). It is interesting that we can measure the distance from north to south, but we can never measure the distance from east to west. There is no record of our failures in heaven. His blood has covered them all. We should all deepen our appreciation of the way God looks at us. His love and acceptance make up the robe we wear. Our Father has given us this robe the same way Jacob gave Joseph the robe of many colors. We should wear it with great confidence and affection for the one who gave us this robe. When He sees us, He sees the robe.

C H A P T E R   1 9

YOUR CREDIT IS GOOD HERE

I WENT TO THE MAILBOX the other day and found some junk mail stating that I was preapproved for a certain credit card. I have no idea how these companies know whether we are creditworthy or not. All I know is that the temptation to find out if we are really qualified for all the credit they are offering is amazing. Wouldn't it be great to find out someday that you have unlimited credit? Think of the things you might purchase. Think of all the vacations you might take and the gifts you could give to others.

I want you to look at righteousness as your credit standing in heaven. The word says that the Father has qualified us to share in the inheritance of the saints in life (Col. 1:12). The Father thus has prequalified you to share His inheritance.

We need to get a deeper understanding of righteousness if we are to press on to maturity. First, we must understand the two categories of righteousness: There is righteous behavior, which includes all the good works that model godliness and holiness. Then there is our righteous character, which is imputed to us by Christ. I want to emphasize our righteous character, or our true righteous standing before God. If we only highlight behavior at the expense of character, our pursuit of righteous living can turn into the law. Many of us pursue right behavior, hoping to solidify our righteous standing. This is a trap of the enemy and the foundation of all religion.

Christianity is living from the inside out, not the outside in. Our lives should manifest the life of Christ that is in us. Some people conclude that if you emphasize character over behavior, you are minimizing holiness and godliness. The truth is that if we know who we are and are secure in our standing before God, we will want to please Him in all aspects of our lives. The Apostle Paul's biggest challenge was from the Jews, who wanted the Christians to conform to the law (the outside) to validate their standing with God (the inside).

Consider Paul's final summation in the book of Galatians: "Circumcision doesn't mean a thing to me. The only thing that matters is living by the transforming power of this wonderful new created life. And all those who live in agreement with this standard will have true peace and God's delight, for they are the true Israel of God" (Gal. 6:15–16, TPT).

The writer of the book of Hebrews laments the lack of progress he sees in the church and its deficient understanding of righteousness. Reflect on his concern for these saints:

> For though by this time you ought to be teachers, you have need again for someone to teach you the elementary principles of the oracles of God, and you have come to need milk and not solid food. For everyone who partakes only of milk is not accustomed to *the word of righteousness*, for he is an infant. But solid food is for the mature, who because of practice have their senses trained to discern good and evil. (Heb. 5:13-14, emphasis mine)

What exactly did the writer mean when he said that they were unfamiliar with the word of righteousness? It seems as if this should be a basic concept for most believers. Some commentators believe the writer was talking about doctrine or deeper truths of the gospel, but that doesn't seem to make sense from the context here. I believe what he is saying is that there must be a fuller comprehension of righteousness than just the righteousness that is imputed to us when are born again and justified by faith. Paul alludes to this in Romans 1:16–17: For I am not ashamed of the gospel, for it is the power of God for salvation to everyone who believes, to the Jew first and also to the Greek. For in it the righteousness of God is revealed *from faith to faith*, as it is written, "BUT THE RIGHTEOUS man SHALL LIVE BY FAITH."

Our understanding of righteousness needs to increase "from faith to faith" to propel us to maturity. This deeper understanding of righteousness then becomes the solid food the writer of Hebrews talks about. A limited understanding of righteousness will result in a limited Christian life.

Hoping to expand their understanding of righteousness, the writer of Hebrews began by talking about Melchizedek (Heb. 7:1–10). He was the individual whom Abraham met when he returned from defeating the kings (Gen. 14:17–24). He then revealed the two names of Melchizedek as the King of Righteousness and the King of Salem, meaning King of Peace. Christ, who is a priest in the likeness of Melchizedek, now carries both these titles. He is our peace and our continual revelation of righteousness.

How exactly is this revelation accomplished? Jesus is now our high priest who continually makes intercession for us. He is our advocate with the Father, reminding God of our true righteous standing because of His perfect sacrifice. This guarantees our secure standing before God. We can now approach the throne of grace with complete confidence because we carry the righteousness of Christ. Like Jesus, we are now the beloved sons and daughters of God who live under an open heaven and can manifest the life of Christ here on earth.

Next we have the Holy Spirit, who is commissioned with bringing us into the truth. The apostle Paul speaks of His ministry in this way: "But the Holy Spirit convinces us that we have received by faith the glorious righteousness of Christ" (Gal. 5:5, TPT). It is the constant reassurance of our righteousness that we need to maintain our constant communion with our Father in heaven. This confidence inspires and propels us to walk in righteousness and bring heaven to earth.

The ministry of the Spirit and the ministry of righteousness are also the work of the Holy Spirit. In Paul's second letter to the Corinthians, he draws our attention to these twin ministries and to how they are designed to set us free from condemnation, which is the enemy of righteousness:

> But if the ministry of death, in letters engraved on stone, came with glory, so the sons of Israel could not look intently at the face of Moses because of the glory of his face, fading as it was, how will the ministry of the Spirit fail to be even more with glory? For if the ministry of condemnation has glory, much more does the ministry of righteousness abound in glory. For indeed what had glory, in this case has no glory because of the glory that surpasses it. For if that which fades away was with glory, much more that which remains is in glory. (2 Cor. 3:7–11, NASB)

Here Paul contrasts the ministry of death and the ministry of condemnation, which are rooted in the law, with the ministry of the Spirit and the ministry of righteousness, which are rooted in Christ. The focus of the law is on our behavior and on how we all fall short of the glory of God. The focus of Christ is on our freedom and acceptance. This focus is amplified in the following verses: "Where the Spirit of the Lord is, there is liberty" (2 Cor. 3:17) and "that we might become the righteousness of God in Him" (2 Cor. 5:21). The ministry of the Spirit and the ministry of righteousness are the twin pillars of confident Christian living. But is it possible to live a life grounded in freedom and acceptance? The answer is a resounding yes. Jesus did, and He invites us to follow Him on that same path.

The ministry of righteousness will always remind me of who I am. I am now a son and an heir. I am holy, blameless, and without reproach. I am chosen, I am royalty, I am His, and the blood of Jesus has made me perfect. The ministry of condemnation is designed to tell me who I am not. I am not worthy. I am not forgiven. I am not accepted in the beloved. This is why Paul says our covenant in God's amazing grace has greater glory.

Jesus gave us insight into this ministry of the Spirit when He had His last meal with His disciples:

> But I tell you the truth, it is to your advantage that I go away; for if I do not go away, the Helper will not come to you; but if I go, I will send Him to you. And He, when He comes, will convict the world concerning sin, righteousness, and judgment; concerning sin, because they do not believe in Me; and concerning righteousness because I go to the Father and you no longer see Me; and concerning judgment, because the ruler of this world has been judged." (John 16:7–11, NASB)

Take note of the three missions of the Holy Spirit:

1. Concerning sin—designed for the world, because they don't believe.

2. Concerning righteousness—for the church, because He goes to the Father.
3. Concerning judgment—for Satan, who is now judged.

Jesus went to the Father after conquering sin and death and secured our salvation. His victory is now our victory. His righteousness is now our righteousness. The Holy Spirit has been sent to remind and reassure us of that victory and our righteous standing with the Father. Our sin debt has been paid, and sin shall no longer be master over us. If sin no longer masters us, then condemnation should no longer master us. His blood is now our covering and cleanses us from all sin. Concerning the sins that so easily entangle us, we should fix our eyes on Jesus, the writer of Hebrews says. Fix your eyes on Calvary where the power of sin was broken. Fix your eyes on that victory where righteousness is the motivating power in your life. "The righteous *shall live* by faith." You *are* righteous, *now live* by faith in that righteousness. You now have the power to say no to sin and continue to walk in righteousness.

"Laying again a foundation of repentance from dead works" seems to be the focus of many of our churches. This is why many Christians live under a constant sense of condemnation and unworthiness. Each week many saints go to church and hear a message of condemnation with repentance as the only cure. Once we repent, the cure is understanding the word of righteousness. You press on toward maturity with a renewed sense of your righteousness, not with a vow to try harder. Many churches would be content with a room full of the "older brother" type of Christians. They never neglect a command, but neither do they know their identity as sons and daughters. I am so thankful that our heavenly Father is still pursuing us to come home and know the true joy of salvation. Even prodigals who are covered in shame and regret will find a Father who will reestablish their righteous standing and cover them with the robe of righteousness.

When Adam and Eve fell, they went into hiding. God went to find them. The first question He asked them was, "Where are you?" not "What did you do?" He wanted them to know the tragic loss of their perfect standing with Him. The Son of Man came to seek and to find what was lost. What was lost was mankind's perfect standing with the Father. The Father then sent the Son to procure that perfect standing for them on the cross.

Finally, we have this amazing revelation from Paul in Romans 5:17: "For if by the transgression of the one, death reigned through the one, much more those who receive the abundance of grace and of the gift of righteousness will reign in life through the One, Christ Jesus."

Are you reigning in life? Or is life raining on you? I love the way the Amplified Bible states Romans 5:17: "Those who receive [God's] overflowing grace (unmerited favor) and the free gift of righteousness [putting them into right standing with Himself] *reign as kings in life* through the one Man Jesus Christ (the Messiah, the Anointed One)."

Reigning as kings in life is our true potential. This is a picture of us in the garden before the fall. We have unbroken communion with God and dominion here on earth. We can now go out and subdue the earth. With unlimited grace available to us and our perfect standing before Him, we can access whatever promise or grace we need to overcome any issue in life.

At the beginning of this chapter, I wanted you to look at righteousness as your credit standing. You now have unlimited credit to procure any or all of God's resources. Think of yourself entering a shopping mall. You can purchase any item from any store with unlimited credit. What often happens for many Christians is that when we enter the mall, Satan reminds us of some sin and tells us our credit is no good. So we leave the mall promising to improve our credit score. We continually have to fight these lies. Our credit is always good with God. He is the one who has secured our line of credit.

Jesus modeled for us what unbroken fellowship with the Father looked like. By living with His father's approval, Jesus was able to manifest the kingdom for any need He saw. Now we also have the same righteousness as Jesus, and we have the same access to the Father that He has. This is why it is so important to understand these deeper revelations of righteousness.

CHAPTER 20

TIME-SHARES IN THE PROMISED LAND

HAVE YOU EVER GONE TO a time-share presentation? Or, worse yet, have you ever bought a time-share, and do you long to rid yourself that property? The time-share representatives do such an amazing sales job. Everything looks terrific. Everything sounds great. But the bottom line is that you never really own your time-share. All you really buy is time, not property. The temporary never becomes permanent.

I find this same parallel in the church. It is your Father's good pleasure to give us His kingdom, but many of us simply own time-shares in that kingdom. We find ourselves living well below the generous inheritance that the Father has provided. The words "all that I have is yours" (Luke 15:31) remain an elusive dream for many believers. We have occasional triumphs and infrequent breakthroughs. Many of us can testify to amazing visitations from God, but somehow we can never turn those visitations into habitations. In short, our experience of living in the Promised Land is temporary and not permanent. We have let unbelief and the traditions of the church rob us of experiencing the fullness of all His promises.

I would like to share an episode in Mark 8:16–21 between Jesus and his disciples that highlights this point. They began to discuss with one another the fact that they had no bread. And Jesus said this to them,

> "Why do you discuss the fact that you have no bread? Do you not yet see or understand? Do you have a hardened heart?
> "HAVING EYES, DO YOU NOT SEE? And HAVING EARS, DO YOU NOT HEAR? And do you not remember, when I broke the five loaves for the five thousand, how many baskets full of broken pieces you picked up?" They said to Him, "Twelve."
> "When I broke the seven for the four thousand, how many large baskets full of broken pieces did you pick up? And they said to Him, "Seven." And He was saying to them, "Do you not yet understand?"

Notice how Jesus reminds them of what living with a full inheritance looks like. He was God in the flesh, the God of more than enough. But they were acting as if He was the God of not enough. Every need Jesus mentioned was supplied with overflow.

Jesus then asks a series of questions that are designed to make His lifestyle our lifestyle.

Do you not see? This question implies that miracles should affect the way we see life. No need is beyond His power or reach. If nothing is impossible with God, then every need is an opportunity for the kingdom of God to manifest.

Do you not hear? This question implies that we can be tone-deaf to the testimonies of His power. Testimonies are proclamations that God has invaded earth and is more than ready to make His presence known in the needs of mankind. Think of the women with the issue of blood or the Roman centurion. They heard about Jesus, and those reports catapulted their faith to levels that made even Jesus marvel. What do you hear when someone has been healed or provided for in an abundant fashion? Do you feel as if someone just won the faith lottery? Or do you look on it as another invitation for you to make their miracle your miracle?

Do you not remember? This question challenges us not to forget that the kingdom of God is not in word only but with power. A gospel divorced from power leaves no legacy. Our memories of past victories should inspire us to expect victories in every circumstance. Longing for the "good old days" when God used to move is not a kingdom mind-set. He is the same yesterday, today, and forever.

Have you no understanding? The reason God came to earth was to reveal that His kingdom was far superior to any earthly kingdom. Jesus did not come as a great teacher but as God, who is the answer to every human need. Jesus even invited those who had a hard time believing His words to believe in Him based on His works. Nothing was impossible for Him when He walked the earth, and nothing should be impossible for those of us who believe Him today.

Do you have a hardened heart? Do you still resist the fact that God wants to do the miraculous? Has your theology hardened your faith to His supernatural power? Have past disappointments and unanswered prayers turned you into a cynic? Ask Him to renew your faith in His goodness and His power to soften your heart. Don't let your past become your future.

All these questions are designed to wake us up from living our lives with limitations. Every miracle Jesus performed gives us pictures of our potential. Jesus said, "Truly, truly, I say to you, he who believes in Me, the works I do, he will do also and greater works than these he will do; because I go to the Father" (John 14:12). Jesus was declaring that His lifestyle was not beyond our reach but available to all who believe.

A woman came by our booth at one of our evangelistic outreaches and asked for prayer. She asked for me to come over because she wanted to tell me something. She said that she had multiple sclerosis and that when she stopped by our booth the year before, she had been in a wheelchair because she had been unable to walk. We had prayed for her, and immediately she had felt a change in her body. She eventually got out of the wheelchair and was able to walk using a cane. Now she wanted more prayer so she could walk without the cane. I am not only grateful for the Lord healing this woman but I also think of how her testimony will draw even more people to Christ. I once heard someone say that every miracle is pregnant with a hundred miracles. His name and His fame will continue to grow as long as we pursue our inheritance.

I must continually position myself to present Jesus as the answer to every need, no matter how impossible the need, and regardless of the results I see. Unless we are willing to go beyond our fears and our doubts, we shall forever be consigned to living our lives in time-shares. The revelation of Christ in me must be greater than any need I see.

CLAIMING YOUR INHERITANCE

So how do we move into our promised inheritance? Each one of us has testimonies of God meeting our needs in unexpected or miraculous ways. But we are no different from His disciples. They saw the miraculous, but those events did not convert them. Once-and-done miracles rarely convert us. They saw Jesus feed thousands and yet they were still worried about bread. Why do the miracles of yesterday fail to deliver us from the worry that stalks us today? To truly embrace our full inheritance, we need to have our minds renewed. It is by pursuing a promise of God and by overcoming the doubts and disappointments, that our minds are truly converted.

Consider the way Jesus spoke about prayer in Luke 11:1–13. He gives us the key to turning the Promised Land into a permanent habitation:

It happened that while Jesus was praying in a certain place, after He had finished, one of His disciples said to Him, "Lord, teach us to pray just as John also taught his disciples."

And He said to them, "when you pray, say:

'Father, hallowed be your name.

Your Kingdom come.

'Give us each day our daily bread.

'And forgive us our sins,

For we ourselves also forgive everyone who is indebted to us. And lead us not into temptation.'"

Then He said to them, "Suppose one of you has a friend, and goes to him at midnight and says to him, 'Friend, lend me three loaves; for a friend of mine has come from a journey, and I have nothing to set before him'; and from inside he answers and says, 'Do not bother me; the door has already been shut and my children and I are in bed; I cannot get up and give you anything.'

"I tell you, even though he will not get up and give him anything because he is his friend, yet because of his persistence he will get up and give him as much as he needs.

"So I say to you, ask, and it will be given to you; seek and you will find; knock, and it will be opened to you. For everyone who asks, receives; and he who seeks, finds; and to him who knocks, it will be opened.

The key is persistence. It is the pursuit of a promise that opens the Promised Land. How often do we ask and not get discouraged?

How long do we seek when all the evidence is pointing in the opposite direction? How loudly do we knock until we have our miracle? It is the asking, the seeking, and the knocking that unlocks our inheritance. It is here that our minds are renewed. It is here that we take His word, not our circumstance, as the final authority. When we diligently seek Him, then we find our reward. Ask. Seek. Knock. Believe. Persist. These words are not for the fainthearted. But they become our road map to the Promised Land.

When I began to establish a healing culture in our church, I had more failures than success. Yet I knew the Lord wanted me to follow this direction. After nine months of persistent praying, I finally had my breakthrough. Now I see unusual miracles because of that persistence. Recently I came up behind a woman, who was visiting our church, to greet her. She seemed startled, and then she asked her children why I was talking so loudly. I did not know it, but she had been deaf in her right ear for forty years. The moment I touched her, God instantly healed her.

God wants to give us the answer to our prayers, but He also wants our minds renewed in the process. Unfortunately, we value answers more than mind renewal. When we can see this twofold aspect of prayer, we won't be so easily discouraged.

Jesus told another parable about prayer regarding a widow and an unjust judge (Luke 18:1–8). She wanted relief from an opponent, and the judge was unwilling to help. Her persistence eventually wore the judge down, and he gave her relief. I remember being a bit confused about these parables on prayer. At first, Jesus seems to extend an open invitation to pray, and then He tells us that the experience is like approaching an unjust judge or a reluctant friend. I eventually came to realize that only by persisting in prayer would I eventually overcome my unbelief and take God's word over my experience. The good news is that in both parables, the individuals received exactly what they asked for. Only through persistence do we remain rooted in the Promised Land. We will then have the confident expectation that God will deliver on all of His promises.

What we focus on will materialize. If we focus on God's word, then faith will materialize (Rom. 10:17). If we focus on our fears, they will also overtake us. A renewed mind is a mind that remains focused on God's promises. We owe the world a picture of what it is like to have all the resources of heaven available to us. If we are told to pray for His kingdom to come and His will to be done on earth as it is in heaven, then we must learn to access those heavenly resources. Jesus lived that kind of life. He was able to tap into His inheritance for any need. Our challenge is to seek His kingdom so that the resources we need will be added unto us.

Abraham is our model of faith. In Hebrews, it says that through faith and patience he inherited the promises. We also need these two ingredients to access our inheritance. We have to remember that God is our ally in our journey of faith. He is the author and finisher of faith. Look at how many times God helped Abraham believe. He used spoken promises, covenants, visual aids, dreams, angelic encounters, and confident confessions to bring Abraham to a place where his faith became sight. Isaac was born, to the delight of Abraham and Sarah. The Lord is just as faithful in helping you secure your inheritance.

The Lord recently dropped a revelation into my heart to encourage me to seek after more of His kingdom. He simply said to my spirit, "Start at the end." What He was saying is that I often start by focusing on my need versus His abundance. God used this same approach with Abraham. He made Abraham look at the stars and said, "So shall your descendants be." By focusing on the fulfillment of the promise rather than his physical limitations, Abraham succeeded in raising his faith to a new level.

When Jesus fed the five thousand, He did not focus on the five loaves and the two fish or the crowd. He simply looked up to heaven. "Set your minds on things above" is a necessary discipline to lay hold of your destiny. If everything that God has is ours, if we are joint heirs with Jesus, and if we have everything pertaining to life and godliness, then we cannot afford to remain in our time-shares. It is time to possess the land.

This is your season. This is the favorable year of the Lord. God is looking for bold adventurers who will embrace movement and risk to lay claim to their promised land. You can do it. You were made for this!

Remember, He became you, so you could become Him! Don't settle for less.

EPILOGUE

MANY YEARS AGO, THERE WAS a TV game show on which the winner was given five minutes to run through a supermarket and put as many things in the shopping cart as possible. Watching the person run through the store while he or she frantically threw as much food as possible in the cart was hilarious. Usually the person would race back to the meat department, grab expensive steaks and roasts, and then run through every aisle. Toward the end, the winner usually had various items falling out of the cart as they tried to beat the clock. The winner finished the race exhausted but extremely satisfied.

These past few years, I have felt like the winner of that game show. Knowing who I am in Christ and recognizing the rich inheritance that I have in Him has brought me more joy and victories than I can count. I have been racing through His promises, filling up my spiritual cart with as many blessings as possible. The revelations in this book are some of the steaks and roasts on which I have been feasting. I pray these truths feed your hungry soul and make you hungry for even more. The good news is that you don't have just five minutes to fill your cart: you have a lifetime to secure as much of Him and His kingdom as possible.

I truly believe we are on the verge of a new reformation, a reformation of identity. For five hundred years, we have faithfully proclaimed justification by faith as one of the central pillars of the Protestant Reformation. Now we need to proclaim just as loudly the true standing of the believer before a holy and loving God. We must stop defining ourselves by our faults and our failures and confidently proclaim that we are the disciples whom Jesus loves. Then the shackles of condemnation will fall off and we will walk confidently in our new redeemed identity.

THE CHALLENGE

Jesus said that His sheep hear His voice and know His voice (John 10:1–4). I want you to take a few minutes to hear His voice regarding your identity. It is one thing for me to tell you these truths but quite another to hear the voice of your shepherd affirming your identity. I have done this exercise in my own church and have seen amazing results. People with poor self-images have been set free from the lies that have bound them. Others have heard words of love and affirmation that have set their spirits soaring. Hearing from God usually takes the form of spontaneous thoughts that you were not previously thinking. The bible refers to this as the "still small voice."

Find a place where there are no distractions. You may want to take along a pen and some paper. Simply say, "Lord I want to hear your voice." Then I want you to ask Him the following three questions:

1. Lord, how do I see myself?
2. Lord, how do you see me?
3. Lord, what do you want me to do?

After you ask a question, just be still and wait for Him to answer. Then move on to the next question. I know He will answer the questions of His children.

REFERENCES

Bainton, Roland. 1950. *Here I Stand: A Life of Martin Luther.* Nashville, TN: Abingdon Press.

Buck, Roland. 1979. *Angels on Assignment.* New Kensington, PA: Whitaker House.

Müller, George. 1878. *Autobiography of George Müller: A Life of Trust.* New York: Sheldon.

Vine, W. E. 1966. *Expository Dictionary of New Testament Words.* Old Tappan, NJ: Fleming H. Revel.

Ministry Contact Information:
Tim Concannon
e-mail: timconcannon910@gmail.com

Church web page:
www.newbeginningschurchnj.org